Tastes and Tales of a Chef

A Culinary Journey with Mr. A

Joseph Amendola,
CEC, CCE, AAC HOF
Make Time for People.
Compiled by Michael Baskette,
CEC, CCE, AAC

PEARSON

Prentice
Hall

D0061198

Upper Saddle River, New Jersey 07458

Library of Congress Cataloging-in-Publication Data
Amendola, Joseph.
    Tastes and tales of a chef: a culinary journey with Mr. A / Joseph Amendola, Michael
Baskette.
    p. cm.
    ISBN 0-13-172754-0
1. Amendola, Joseph. 2. Cooks—United States—Biography. I. Baskette, Michael. II. Title.
    TX649.A44A3 2006
    641.5'092—dc22

2005015340

Executive Editor: *Vernon R. Anthony*
Editorial Assistant: *Yvette Schlarman*
Managing Editor: *Mary Carnis*
Production Editor: *Emily Bush, Carlisle Publishers Services*
Production Liaison: *Janice Stangel*
Director of Manufacturing and Production: *Bruce Johnson*
Manufacturing Manager: *Ilene Sanford*
Manufacturing Buyer: *Cathleen Petersen*
Creative Director: *Cheryl Asherman*
Cover Design Coordinator: *Miguel Ortiz*
Executive Marketing Manager: *Ryan DeGrote*
Senior Marketing Coordinator: *Elizabeth Farrell*
Marketing Assistant: *Les Roberts*
Cover Design: *Linda Punskovsky*
Cover Image: *Courtesy of Joseph Amendola*

Pearson Education LTD.   Pearson Education Australia PTY, Limited
Pearson Education Singapore Pte. Ltd.   Pearson Education North Asia Ltd.
Pearson Education, Canada, Ltd.   Pearson Educacion de Mexico, S.A. de C.V.
Pearson Education—Japan   Pearson Education Malaysia, Pte. Ltd.

10 9 8 7 6 5 4 3 2
ISBN: 0-13-172754-0

*Dedicated to my beautiful wife
Marge Amendola and our two
blessed children Jeanette and Joseph.*

Contents

Joe's Ten Commandments
TO ENHANCE YOUR CAREER

Do unto others as you want others to do unto you.

Pass on your knowledge and skills to your apprentices.

Maintain good health and diet.

Enjoy your work and free time.

Do things in moderation.

Make time for people.

Don't burn bridges—you may need them.

Have a hobby or hobbies.

Keep learning and refreshing your education.

Plan a financial program for your twilight years.

To Joe Amendola
"MISTER MASTER"

When I think of you, I have to smile
The way you're sailin' all the while. . .
And I feel the welcome you extend
From where you are—to Here, my friend,
You're such a pleasure, Joe, to know.
I thought I'd write and tell you so.
And so, here goes—I'll tell you why
You're my favorite "piece of pie."

You've spent your lifetime in the dough
And you do wear it well, you know;
I'm sure your students will agree
That you're the chef they'd like to be.
You're the kind of man who cares
Just how each student effort fares—
And in your interest and concern,
It's not just baking that they learn.

You keep a very even keel,
A surriness, of great appeal—
And Joe, if you should once complain—
I don't think we could stand the strain!
Your inner strength is something grand.
Tiers above most men, you stand.
You're generous with your time to all
Though time, sometimes, is in shortfall.

And even then, you've written books
To share your skills, in words, for cooks!
I've never seen one do so much
Retaining still, the common touch.
How humble; Joe, a man are you—
Had unimpressed by what you do. . .
(Your head has worn a lot of hats—
Your back deserves a lot of pats.)

You've truly been a cornerstone
In how the C.I.A. has grown. . .
A rightful MASTER of a man
In helping every way you can. . .
And now, again, they count on you
To do the thing you love to do. . .
Developing. . . (still raising dough)
But this time, for new buildings, though.

. . . One knows somehow that you'll succeed
. . . In finding all the funds you'll knead.

From your friend Ray Marshall

Foreword

John of Salisbury spoke long ago about special and exceptional people who, by their leadership and actions and example, pave the way for others to follow when he said:

We are like dwarfs perched upon the shoulders of giants. We see more and farther than our predecessors, not because we have keener vision or greater height, but because we are lifted up and borne aloft on their gigantic stature.

Joe Amendola, I think surely fits this observation to a "T." He is one of several giants of the Culinary Institute of America.

I first encountered Joe Amendola in the early 1960s. As a result of the Second Vatican Council called by Pope John XXII to modernize Catholic institutions, special education had become a priority.

I was assigned to develop foodservice programs for Catholic institutions. Someone had recommended that I contact Joe Amendola at the Culinary Institute of America, then in New Haven, Connecticut. I had little, if any, experience in developing a syllabus for this specialized education.

I visited Joe at the Culinary Institute to discuss this situation with him. Joe listened attentively to my predicament and then suggested a course of study for our summer short courses. Thus began a relationship that has lasted over forty-five years.

Joe assisted in setting up programs in baking and food preparation with Chef Jim Bernni and Chef Louis Bartenbach. At that time we felt that our foodservice personnel were receiving the best practical foodservice education possible. During the next fifteen years, Joe and his colleagues dedicated themselves to this educational work with great enthusiasm and dedication.

The Catholic institutions are indebted to Joe Amendola. We were blessed with a person of his caliber, experience, and initiative.

Joe Amendola served in many major administrative positions at the Culinary Institute of America during his nearly fifty-year tenure. He had a keen perception of selecting the right person for a particular position.

During the summer workshops for the nuns, we hired college students from Stonehill College. When Wayne Berning was in his junior year, I assigned him to Joe Amendola. At the end of the summer, Joe asked me to let him know when Wayne graduated. He stated that Wayne was the type of professional young person that would do well at the CIA. Wayne was ultimately hired at CIA and performed in various administrative positions for a decade.

In conclusion, Joe Amendola was indeed a role model for the younger generation of chefs and bakers. He has made an extraordinary contribution to the foodservice industry.

Brother Herman Zaccarelli, CSC

Tastes and Tales of a Chef

A Culinary Journey with Mr. A

Joe at age 9 working in his uncle's bakery, Lucibbella's.

A Fifty-Dollar Deal Lasted a Lifetime

Growing up in the 1920s in New Haven, Connecticut, as one of nine children in a household with only a moderate income was nothing like you might imagine it today. But it formed the eleven of us (counting my mom and dad) into a tight-knit group where everyone knew their place in the family and shared responsibilities without question. Of course my father and mother had something to say about that too.

It's hard for me to remember a time where there were no telephones, radios, refrigerators, central air or heating systems, nevermind washing machines, dryers, televisions, electronic games, computers, and all the other luxuries we take for granted these days, but that's the way it was in my house when I was a boy. We didn't know how poor we were, but we made the most of what we had and were grateful for whatever we were given.

You've probably heard similar stories, but I lived when there were no buses to take us to school. Walking to school was not an option; it was the only way of getting there. Kids today may have to wait outside for their bus to pick them up, and I'm sure it gets awfully cold sometimes, but my brothers and I would have longed for such a ride no matter how long we had to wait in the cold or rain or anything else. There were no buses coming to pick us up, and neither mom nor dad had a car that they could take us in. Besides, walking to school was good exercise and you got to talk to your friends the whole way without some bus driver telling you to sit down and behave. It might have been a harder way of living, but it forged us all into a stronger family who never took anything for granted and always looked for a better way of doing things.

In the evenings, and only after our homework and chores were done, our father would gather us all together in the living room to tell us our short nightly story. More often than not it would be a religious story or at least a story with a moral or message behind it. It was my dad's way of teaching us to get along with each other and make something of ourselves.

There weren't any Mickey Mouse or Cat in the Hat stories to read under the blankets either; in fact we didn't even have blankets, not like the blankets we have today. In those days flour and sugar came in 100-pound cotton sacks. My mother would take them apart, wash out the ink printing, and make pillow cases, bed sheets, and even some of our clothes out of them. Oh yes, we were lucky enough to have a Singer sewing machine, which mom used everyday to make or repair what bed linens and clothing we had.

Then, in the winter months, when the bed was too cold to climb into, we would put a brick in the coal-burning stove we used to heat the house and cook on. When the brick was hot, we would wrap it in a towel and place it in the bed by our feet. What a delight that was, to have warm toes when trying to sleep with three or four brothers all on the same bed!

My mother was also an excellent cook and baker who prepared great pots of food for all of us as well as anyone visiting our home. No matter how poor we might have been, I always remember my mother having plenty of food to place on the table. You must remember that everything was homemade, so a dollar went a lot farther in feeding us than it would today. One of my mom's daily routines was to mix and knead batches of bread dough after she had cleaned the whole kitchen from dinner (we would all help) and before going to bed and let it rise overnight; that way she could get up early in the morning and have hot bread for our breakfast as we got up for school and my dad got up for work.

My father had an old rowboat (sounds funny saying it was an old boat, eighty years later) and he would go fishing on the weekends in the harbor (New Haven Harbor) or one of a dozen small lakes, ponds, and rivers nearby. He would often have to paddle as many as six to eight miles by himself before he could catch enough fish for our table. That became almost a weekly activity for him, for we ate fish every Friday. Free fish, even though it took work to get it, was a lot better than paying for fish with the little money we had.

Dad also made his own wine, which included crushing of the grapes (guess who helped?) and preparing the wine barrels. Mom and all of us kids would be busy all summer long canning tomatoes, tomato sauce, green beans, eggplant, and a host of other vegetables we would buy in bulk (to save a penny) and clean, cut, and can so that we would have enough for the entire year. We often made so much we would end up giving some of it away as presents to family and friends. Those were the kinds of gifts people really appreciated back then, gifts made with your own hands and for a special need—nourishment. We even roasted our own coffee beans.

All the children had to go to work at an early age to help out with the growing expenses. The girls would get jobs as seamstresses (they got a lot of practice at home) and many of the boys would get jobs at the corner barber shop, shining shoes for customers, or at the neighborhood store, bagging groceries. I was the lucky one, for at the age of nine I was placed as a baking apprentice with my uncle, who had started an Italian and French pastry shop, Lucibello's, named after my grandmother, in New Haven in 1929.

Somehow my mother had been able to save up a few dollars, one penny at a time, and offered to loan my uncle fifty dollars so he could buy enough flour and sugar to help start the bakery. Fifty dollars went a long way back then; it paid for enough products to get my uncle started, and then fresh-baked sweet buns, cakes, and pies kept the customers coming.

My uncle also needed help to make the dough, clean the bakeshop, and sell baked goods to the customers, so, along with the fifty dollars, I was sent to help him. So I guess you might say that fifty-dollar deal lasted a lifetime, for I've been in the foodservice business ever since.

Being a bakery apprentice was not a glamorous job; even though I was working for my uncle, he didn't give me any slack. Instead he seemed to push me even harder than he did the other workers, probably because he knew he could get away with it. There was no way I was going to go home and complain to my mother or father that work was hard; they would have just said something like . . . "Good, keep it up."

I washed all the pots and pans (and that was before there were sheet pan liners and spray vegetable oils, which make it a lot easier to do so today) at the bakery, carried coal to a coal bin that was used to fuel the huge baking ovens, swept the floors, greased and dusted cake pans, and ran all types of errands for my uncle and the other bakers. One of my jobs was to place cherries on cookies for hours upon hours. I did everything that other workers did not want to do, but it taught me discipline and the right and wrong way to do things.

I remember one occasion when, after sweeping the floors a thousand times or so, the straw on the bottom of the long, brown wooden handle was wearing thin and had shifted to an extreme 45-degree angle, which made it even more difficult to do an already tedious job. So I was given twenty-five cents to go and buy a new broom; my uncle was not happy, but there was a lesson to learn. Upon my quick return from the store I was given a demonstration on how to properly sweep the floor. Yes, there is a right and wrong way to do everything, and floor sweeping, I was soon to learn, was no different. To properly sweep and to ensure that you can get the most out of your broom, you should sweep with only three strokes while holding the broom one way and then turn the handle of the broom and sweep three strokes the other way. In that way the straw will wear out evenly, giving a good solid work area for the entire life of the broom (until all the straw is worn so thin that the old broom has to be replaced). Yes, there is a right and a wrong way of doing practically everything.

The longer I worked there the more I was able to learn the basics of the different recipes used for all the pastry products we made. It took many years, but I did become quite proficient in every aspect of running my uncle's bakery. So, even with all the great cooking and baking schools available today, I feel that my apprenticeship training was the best I could have hoped for.

I've been in the foodservice business now for over seventy-five years, and am proud of and grateful for my training and experience, no matter how hard it was at the time. It was all the hard work and discipline that I experienced that gave me the skills to enable my success in later years.

Bavarian Creams
(15 servings)

Ingredients

1 qt.	Milk
6	Egg yolks
8 oz.	Sugar
1/2 oz.	Gelatin, unflavored
1 pt.	Heavy cream, whipped

Method

1. Heat the milk.
2. Beat together egg yolks, sugar, and gelatin. Add to milk (Step 1). Do not boil. Cool.
3. Whip cream and fold into above mixture (Step 2) after it has cooled and started to thicken.
4. Place in a mold or cup and allow to set until firm. Unmold and serve with sauce.

Meringue Shells
(50 shells)

Ingredients

1 lb.	Egg whites
2 lb.	Granulated sugar

Method

1. Whip together egg whites and 1 lb. granulated sugar to a stiff peak.
2. Fold the second pound of sugar into above mixture, using a minimum amount of motion.

Tube into desired shapes using pastry bag and star tip.
Baking Temperature: Bake dry (about 1 hr.) at 250°F.
Remarks: For variation, 4 oz. of granulated nuts or chocolate bits or melted chocolate may be folded in.

Meringue Glacé

1. Line a baking pan with paper. Fit a pastry bag with a star tube and fill with meringue mixture. Dress out rosettes or ovals.
2. Sprinkle with fine granulated sugar, and follow instructions for Meringue Shells.
3. To serve: Press a meringue rosette or oval on each side of a scoop of ice cream. Garnish with whipped cream.

Schaum Torte

1. Line a baking pan with paper. Trace four 8 in. circles.
2. Fit a pastry bag with a plain 3/8 in. tube and fill with meringue mixture.
3. Completely cover one circle with meringue using a spiral design.
4. Outline two of the circles with meringue about 1 1/2 in. wide and 1 in. thick.
5. On the final circle press out a ring of "kisses" with a star tube. Each kiss must touch the one next to it. This will form a wreath of meringue kisses.
6. Dry in oven at 250°F for about 1 hr. Cool and remove from paper.
7. Place the solid meringue circle on a cool serving platter.
8. Place the two outlined circles on top of the solid circle.
9. Fold 1 pt. of sliced strawberries that have been soaked in liqueur into 1 pt. of heavy cream that has been whipped.
10. Fill the meringue shell with this mixture and place the wreath of meringue kisses on top. Garnish with a whole strawberry.

Lemon Angel Filling
(for two 9 in. pies)

Ingredients

5 oz.	Lemon juice
6 oz.	Egg yolks (8)
12 oz.	Sugar
1/4 oz.	Salt
1/4 oz.	Gelatin
1 qt.	Heavy cream, whipped
2 9 in.	Meringue pie shells
	Chocolate shavings

Method

1. Simmer lemon juice, egg yolks, sugar, salt, and gelatin together ingredients for 30 min. Remove from heat. Cool.
2. Fold whipped heavy cream into mixture in Step 1.
3. Fill pie shells with filling.
4. Decorate top of pie with chocolate shavings.

I can see what you're up to with one eye open. He's not really playing "I Spy" simply getting it across that he is well aware of what's going on, and will not be fooled. (From Joe Amendola's book *More Than Words Can Express*, unpublished)

From the Backs of Donkeys

As I stated earlier, my uncle was a task master who gave me no preferential treatment even though it was my mother who had helped him open his pastry shop in New Haven with that now famous fifty-dollar loan. That was okay with me, for I was eager to learn everything I could, and I knew there was no better place to begin my training than at the bottom of the totem pole.

At Lucibello's we made everything from scratch, including ice cream, sorbets, and all forms of pastries, cakes, and pies. We even made our own candied orange peel—a delicious confection with all the natural flavors of fresh orange that we used as decorative garnishes for many of our specialty desserts. This was done by peeling the skins off of the oranges, one of my jobs, scraping off as much of the white inner membrane as possible, cutting the peel into thin slivers, and then boiling them in a simple syrup made by boiling one part sugar and one part water until it reaches a semi-thick consistency. These candied orange peels were a delight for the kids who used to buy a handful of them for a nickel, they ate them just like candy, but they were a healthy, delicious snack.

This was during the time that produce vendors would carry their goods through the streets of New Haven in carts drawn by donkeys and horses, calling out their offerings as they canvassed the streets. "Blueberries . . . strawberries . . ." came the call, and my uncle would send me outside to wave the vendor over to the back of the bakery to bargain over his goods.

Vendors would carry and sell anything that was in season: blueberries and strawberries in the spring and early summer, which we used for pie fillings, turnovers, and ice creams; watermelons in the summer, used for sorbets and cool summer drinks; and pumpkins and apples in the fall, used for pies and apple or pumpkin butter. This is also how we got our oranges later in the winter—they made their way all the way from Florida or California to Connecticut and other northern cities—and bananas from South America arrived in New Haven after an even longer trip by boat, then train, then by horse- or donkey-drawn cart.

My uncle would always be the one to bargain down the price, and he was adept at getting the price as low as he could. I learned the trick of negotiation from him without him even knowing I was paying attention.

Naturally, anything and everything he purchased would become my responsibility to peel, chop, or otherwise get ready for the bakers in my uncle's shop, who turned them magically into a whole assortment of scrumptious desserts. Their creativity was always interesting to watch, and taste, as they seemed to have a certain intuition when it came to selecting the right fruit for the particular dessert.

What I learned most of all was that you had to "make do" with what you had to work with. Your option was simple: Whatever the produce vendors carried on the backs of donkeys you would have to use in your bakeshop. If the cart didn't have strawberries it would likely have grapes, cherries, or raspberries. If not apples it would carry plums, tangerines, and pears. Perhaps it was because we didn't have an alternative, but using fruits in season made baking and pastry production seem more fun and adventurous to us all.

For one thing, we didn't have to worry about changing our bakery offerings once a month or once a quarter as a lot of places have to do today to keep their customers excited. The items changed with the seasons whether we wanted them to or not. Every day the bakery case was exciting, offering a different assortment of pastries, pies, tarts, and cakes practically every week.

There's still nothing like fresh fruit picked at the height of its season for pie and pastry fillings and toppings. It didn't matter that we couldn't get some things when they were out of season, there was always something to choose from that could be utilized in the bakery.

We also would buy our own lemons and limes for their juice (guess who had to squeeze them all?), which we would use for everything from meringue pies to icings and fillings. Whole bushels would be bought at the same time to get the right price, and I would spend hours upon hours preparing them for storage (lemon and lime juice would last for weeks) or for immediate use by the bakers. I didn't mind all the work. After all, it kept me close to where the bakers were doing their magic in preparing the various pastry doughs, cake batters, icings, fillings, pies, and tarts. And if I promised to clean especially well when they were done, they would often toss me a sweet dessert for my efforts.

In the bakeshop there were few, if any, paper products available for purchase—no sheet pan liners, no cardboard cake circles. So another of my daily jobs, on top of everything else, was to grease and flour the sheet pans and cut cardboard cake circles out of the boxes our other supplies came in. But I didn't really mind; it kept me busy, and time does fly by when you are busy, and brought me closer and closer to the baking production that fascinated me. Over the eight years that I worked there I was able to learn a lot of the basic procedures and recipes the expert bakers used to make their mixed array of bakery and pastry products just by watching and helping out where I could.

Probably the most time-consuming project I had when working for my uncle's pastry shop was making the jams and jellies the bakers used for doughnut filings, cake accents, and torte-layering syrups out of the fresh fruit he would buy from the produce street vendors.

One day, after spending hours peeling, slicing, and cooking some fruit for one of the pastry shop's most used jams, apricot jam, I decided to ask my uncle for the next day off. I had not had a single day off, not even weekends or holidays (on holidays the bakery was even more busy than usual, so no one on the staff could take off), for over eight years, and I thought it was time to take one. I can't remember what it is I wanted to do that day, but I knew I needed to be off, and didn't hesitate to ask my uncle.

To my surprise my uncle didn't even form a wrinkle on his brow when he looked straight into my eyes and said, "You spoiled little boy [I was seventeen years old by then], if you want one day off you'll want another later. Instead take them all off; you are fired."

The shock of getting fired lasted only a few seconds, and then I was actually happy he let me go. I remember running home from the bakery that day with a big smile on my face. I wasn't just happy to be released from the seven-days-a-week schedule I had worked for the past several years, but for the opportunities I knew existed for me.

I probably would have stayed working for my uncle for several more years, slowly making my way up the ladder to baker's helper, bench worker, and then finally to baker and finisher if it were up to him. I felt obligated to do what I was told, and never once thought myself better than others, or that I wasted my time there. Being fired released me from my obligation and gave me the opportunity to go out and look for a better job, which, in the growing New Haven restaurant and bakery industry, was not hard to do.

I was working two days later in a bigger bakery that produced a full assortment of breads and rolls in addition to the sweet buns, cookies, doughnuts, cakes, puff pastry, choux paste (for éclairs and cream puffs), and Danish dough products that my uncle's shop produced. When I took the job at Gilbert's Bakery, still in New Haven, I was happy and challenged to learn all over again, and this time in the position of baker.

I had finally passed my apprenticeship, and getting fired helped me to realize that it was time to move on. Sometimes people tend to become complacent in their lives and their jobs, as I had done. By forcing me to change, my uncle taught me one of the most important lessons of my youth. Don't wait for an opportunity to come knocking on your door; when you have achieved your goals by working in one place, move on to another, and another, for the sake of learning, networking, and building a stronger repertoire of experiences and knowledge.

Nonetheless, today I discourage students and other young culinarians from jumping from job to job. It does not look good on a resumé, where dedication is one of the professional traits the best houses look for in a new employee, and limits learning, for you can only scratch the surface of what that house, and the people working in it, can teach you over time. Stay with a job for at least a year or two to absorb as much training and knowledge as you can before moving on to another, and you will learn to improve your craft and your professional posture with precision and thoroughness.

I still took the next day off after my uncle fired me, as planned.

Crepes
(20 servings)

Ingredients

8	Whole eggs
1 qt.	Water
1/2 oz.	Salt
4 oz.	Cornstarch (1 c.)
4 oz.	Flour (1 c.)
4 oz.	Butter, melted

Method

1. Mix and blend eggs and water. Add salt.
2. Gradually add cornstarch and flour. Blend well.
3. Add to mixture in Step 2. Blend.
4. Heat an ungreased pan. Ladle in batter, rolling and turning pan so entire surface is thinly covered. Sauté without coloring. Turn. Set other side without coloring.
5. Place a small amount of granulated sugar in pan. Allow to caramelize while pressing with back of a spoon. Add 2 pats of butter and juice or rind of 1 lemon. Add crepes. Baste with liquid and fold. De-glaze pan with brandy. Flame. Plate crepes and pour sauce over them.

Remarks: A mix of 1 qt. liquid makes about 60 crepes. To store, cover with waxed paper or foil and refrigerate. If crepes tend to stick while sautéing, pan may be wiped occasionally with a cloth dipped in melted butter. Use just enough to produce a light coating. This should be done only when absolutely necessary.

Variations:

Suzette—Basic orange, flamed with Grand Marnier liqueur and cognac.

Rosemary—Basic orange with peach, red cherries; flamed with Curacao.

Cinzano (Kirsch)—Basic lemon-orange, flamed with Cinzano and Kirsch.

Copacabana—Basic coffee with hazlenut puree, flamed with Kahlua.

Hawaienne—Basic orange with pineapple cubes.

Georgina—Stuffed with diced pineapple, flamed with Curacao.
Normande—Stuffed with stewed apples, diced; flamed with Calvados.
Napolitaine—Stuffed with a little orange marmalade, flamed with Curacao.
Maltaise— Orange-lemon, flamed with Curacao.
Suchard—Basic crepe with chocoate, flamed with Crème de Cacao
San Juan—Basic crepe, flamed with rum.
Summertime—Basic crepe; add lemon, orange, or any fruit-flavored sherbet.
Virgin Islands—Basic crepe; add bananas and rum.

Strawberries à La Ritz (Fraises à La Ritz)
(8 servings)

Ingredients

1 qt.	Strawberries
	Sugar (to sweeten)
1/4 c.	Anisette
3 oz.	Flour
8 oz.	Sugar
4	Eggs
1 qt.	Boiling milk
8 oz.	Heavy cream (1 c.)

Method

1. Put well-sugared strawberries in a bowl. Pour the Anisette liqueur over them. Leave in refrigerator for 1 or 2 hr. until well chilled.
2. Blend flour, sugar, and eggs together. Slowly dilute with boiling milk and cook for a few minutes. Stir constantly until mixture boils. Let cool.
3. Add well-beaten cream and gently mix in strawberries and juice (Step 1).

Remarks: Add a little red coloring if necessary to give mixture a pink color. A few large strawberries can be arranged as a garnish on top. Serve very cold.

Linzer Dough for Tortes or Slices
(50 servings)

Ingredients

1 lb.	Butter
1 lb.	Sugar
8	Eggs
1	Lemon rind
1/8 oz.	Nutmeg
1/8 oz.	Cinnamon
1 lb.	Nut powder
3 lb.	Pastry flour

Method

1. Cream together butter and sugar.
2. Add eggs gradually.
3. Add lemon rind, nutmeg, cinnamon, nut powder, and pastry flour and mix into a dough.
4. Refrigerate before rolling.

Reader's Notes and Thoughts

Aw, get lost.w The upward thrust of the hand meaning "go away, I'm not interested." Many a court lady might have used this gesture to a too amorous suitor in days of yore. (From Joe Amendola's book *More Than Words Can Express*, unpublished)

The Machine Got Used to the Bakers

The foodservice and hospitality industries have seen tremendous improvements in technology over the last four hundred years, leading cooks and bakers to learn new skills and knowledge constantly throughout their long careers. We may think technology is changing fast today, but we're not the first generation of people to make that claim. Many of the tools, equipment, and ingredients we take for granted in modern kitchens and bakeshops today were at one time new and exciting changes that transformed the industry one step at a time.

Just imagine the excitement surrounding the introduction of single-service cookware in the fourteenth century. Taillevent (c. 1310–1395), a chef in the kitchens of King Philip VI of France, must have thought culinary artistry had reached its pinnacle of perfection when he had adapted all he had learned from before to the new technology of small pots and pans.

Before this momentous change took place, metals were not yet pliable enough to make thin, bowl-shaped pots and pans, forcing cooks to cook meats and poultry either over open flame (or burning charcoal) stabbed through by large, rounded spears suspended over the direct heat, or in large cauldrons that took a long time to heat up and were impractical for small-quantity cooking.

Now imagine, if you can, especially those of you who are already cooking and baking, working in a large, open kitchen with extremely high ceilings and no fans, but with massive chimneys cut into the roof at various intervals throughout the canopy to exhaust the heat and the fumes: Open-pit barbecues make up the cook's line; bakers are using wood-fired brick ovens for their artisan breads and simple desserts; meat is hanging and being butchered in close proximity to the cooks for easy access as business demanded.

Those cooks and bakers experienced a miracle in technology when they were able to enclose those hot, open fires in cast-iron ovens and cook, on the tops and in the bellies of those ovens, using pots and pans that would hold smaller portions than were ever cooked before. The excitement they must have felt could only rival inspirational emotions, for the great chefs took pleasure in adapting old methods and creating new dishes using the new technology that they witnessed being born.

Thousands of other miracles have been happening ever since. Look, for example, at the new technology Louis Pasteur was exploring in his Parisian chemistry lab that changed forever the way we think of food deterioration and those pesky tiny organisms (microorganisms) that both benefit (as in cheese production, bread fermentation, and yogurt, sour cream, and buttermilk processing) and harm the foods we eat—Pasteur's explorations led to the pasteurization process we take for granted today. Pasteur was a pioneer, and his discoveries were revolutionary for his day.

I can't imagine the days before industrial scientists in the late nineteenth century developed baking soda (sodium bicarbonate) for the first time, which then quickly became a staple ingredient in bakeshops around the world. A large amount of what we consider everyday bakery and pastry items were not possible without this new advent in technology. Quick breads, biscuits, muffins, pan cakes, cookies, and crackers were new inventions of that era, and even cakes expanded their types by leaps and bounds as they were no longer dependent on high amounts of sugar and fat for leavening (the old pound cake formula required equal amounts of sugar, fat, eggs, and flour for its firm, buttery texture and taste). The repertoire of the baker and pastry chef expanded exponentially in a matter of a few years.

In my day I have seen the commercial use of refrigeration become commonplace and the advent of proofing cabinets, table-top mixers, blenders, convection ovens, and portable heat (Heat Cell and Sterno are well-recognized brands). In the bakeshop I have witnessed the introduction of emulsified shortening and margarine; all-purpose flour was not available when I learned my craft, yet I continued to learn as these things became available. I personally had a hand in developing frozen pastry dough, which has alleviated all the production time it used to take to make these doughs on-premise for large-volume producers. All these things were new at one time and challenged the ingenuity, creativity, and stamina for change and progress of the cook and the baker.

Yet with all the excitement and innovation that comes with these new technologies, there are those who resist change and stand on tradition and classic techniques for their stern posture against anything new. Let me tell you of one such story where well-learned bakers were intimidated by new technology and afraid of what it would mean to their entire careers should they be forced to embrace it.

I was the supervising bakery manager of Gilbert's Bakery in New Haven just prior to my military adventures, which you will read about later, when the owner Anton Bosch purchased a revolutionary new dough-cutting and dough-rolling machine for the bakery. There were twenty-eight trained, very traditional bakers under my direction, many of whom were trained under strict apprenticeships in Germany and other European countries. They were not always open to my directions, let alone my suggestions on how they might improve their skills and techniques.

The new machine promised to help expand our product line by taking away some of the menial duties of hand cutting and rolling the hundreds of different rolls we made in the large ovens every day. Freeing the bakers of the time it took to do those daily tasks would allow them the extra time to create new and better product lines for the retail cases. Unfortunately, they didn't see it that way.

The Germans were accustomed to using the popular Duchess press to cut pre-weighed dough into individual portions for rounding, yet they insisted on rounding the rolls by hand as they had done thousands of times before to produce the nice, round, uniform rolls their reputation was based on. When they saw the workmen bringing in the big machine, they did everything they could to get in the way without stopping the progress all together, with folded arms and gruff demeanor.

After the workmen had finally gotten the machine in place and retreated from the fiery glare that must have been burning in their backs, the bakers went back to work without even asking a question or attempting to understand the magnitude of the change that was sitting there on the floor, staring at them as they were hard at work at their benches.

I tried to explain to them the true reason why the owner had purchased the machine—to free up some of the daily time they invested in menial activities so that that time could be used to produce greater and better products—but they wouldn't hear a word of what I was saying. They were convinced that the machine would do all the work they had done and they would soon find themselves without jobs. How could the owner afford such a machine as this one, and still pay them all the wages they were used to getting?

No matter what I said or did, they even refused to come close to the machine and became more angry and defiant the more I tried to coax them. So I went to the owner, Mr. Bosch, and asked his advice.

My boss was a seasoned bakery chef himself, and had owned and operated the bakery for dozens of years, watching it grow bigger and better each season. He was genuinely a stern man, but a man of morals and dignity. He let me into his office and asked me to explain what the problem was that I was having difficulty dealing with.

I told him that in spite of my trying to convince the others that the new cutting and rolling machine would save them valuable time so that they could spend that time making more beautiful desserts, I could not shake their fear that it was really an attempt to do away with them altogether. Because of that fear they clung together as a group, so not one of them would even approach the machine to try it out.

I almost expected the owner to get up from his desk right away and storm out of the room into the bakery to confront the Germans face to face. I could almost see him brushing past the dough benches so quickly that flour dust soared through the air and rolling pins went rolling. I could almost hear him speaking to them in German so there could be no confusion of the orders he would surely be giving to force them to use the new machine and be happy about it. He's made a similar speech many times to the bakers and me—a quick lesson on doing things right away and doing so correctly the first time.

Yet instead of an abrupt "they said what?" kind of attitude, he actually laughed a bit and leaned back in his chair, making no attempt to stand up, with a grin that slowly spread from cheek to cheek.

"So, they're afraid they're going to lose their jobs?" he asked me. I said again that I couldn't understand why, on account of how wonderful the new machine looked and how much faster it would make their work go.

"You see, Joseph," he said to me, still smiling, "it's not the machine at all that scares them, but they fear their jobs are at stake. Look at what the true problem is, before you try to fix it. Let's prove to them that we need both the new machine and them to make this bakery an even bigger success for all of us tomorrow."

So then he said to me, "Instead of asking the bakers to get used to using the new machine, forcing them to comply with the new technology, let the machine, instead, get used to the bakers."

I admit I must have been scratching my head by then, wondering what he was going to say next. How were we supposed to get a machine used to people?

This is what he said: "Do not say another word about the new machine. Let them go on about their business doing their duties the same way they've done it for years. You, Joseph, I want you to start working on the machine as though it were yours, and yours alone. Don't say anything to the others, and watch what happens."

So I did what I was told. The next day I went about my job just as I did every day and didn't even mention the machine to the bakers as they came in to work. We set up production schedules as normal, discussed all the specialty products we needed, and then went about our business getting the jobs done that were needed to fill the bakery cases and the wholesale deliveries that were quickly expanding.

When I had finished my normal management duties of planning the day's activities, taking inventory of the goods on hand, and passing the order information to the owner, I went about getting ready to make a large batch of soft rolls for a special order I neglected to tell the other bakers about. Naturally I collected all my ingredients, made my dough as I had done a hundred times before, and then shimmied up to the new, shiny machine to begin the process of weighing, cutting, and rolling.

Within forty minutes I was able to cut and roll over five hundred rolls using the machine, which hummed along in perfect unison with the blenders and mixers on tables and floors around the bakery. One tray at a time I slowly filled one, two, three, even four speed racks with newly shaped rolls in only a couple of hours of work.

I still didn't say anything to the other bakers. I neither boasted of my success with using the new machine nor chastised them for their arrogant defiance in choosing not to use the machine. I simply cleaned up my work area, rolled the racks to the area of the bakeshop where they would rest and proof, and went about finishing my other duties for the day.

I repeated the same scenario the next day, and the next after that. For two weeks I worked the machine by myself, rolling hundreds and hundreds of rolls made from plain dough, which were later used for dinner rolls, and sweet dough, used for hot cross buns, without breaking a sweat. Still neither I nor the bakery owner said one word to the other bakers about the machine.

It was just prior to Easter that year when the machine was brought in, and the bakers were faced with making thousands of hot cross buns, as they had done every year before, by hand. Hot cross buns are sweet buns with white icing piped on the top of the finished roll in the shape of a thin cross to commemorate the crucifixion and resurrection of Jesus, according to the huge Roman Catholic population surrounding our bakery. In addition to an expanded entourage of sweet buns, turnovers, pies, doughnuts, and cakes with way too many orders to count, hot cross buns routinely became our number-one seller every Easter season.

One day I was busy going about doing my own work and hardly paid attention to the other bakers who seemed to be busy making their usual batches of plain and sweet yeast dough for the morning production. They were making extra-large amounts of the dough than usual, but I knew our orders would be up all week. I couldn't wait to use the new machine later that afternoon, and wondered if the old Germans ever would.

That day something must have happened earlier that I was not aware of, probably over their first cup of coffee, but it seemed as though no real discussion took place among the Germans. Then, all of a sudden, instead of one or two of the bakers staying back to dust the tables and get the racks ready for their roll production, they all headed toward the new machine. Within minutes the machine was humming, and I don't remember any other noise in the entire bakeshop at that same moment.

Not a word was spoken the rest of the day, other than a little mumbling under the breath, which I always thought was normal. Yet the German bakers used the machine every day after that, as though they had been doing so for years.

I guess my boss was right not to force the bakers to use the machine, for it would have caused a great deal more frustration and consternation than was necessary. Some of them may have even quit the bakery rather than sacrifice their pride or get fired, which they all feared. What they learned quickly (they must have forgotten) was that if any one of us were to leave just days prior to the busy Easter season, it would have been worse for the rest of us. There was no chance of losing their jobs, and this realization made them work even harder.

Instead of forcing the machine on the bakers, we allowed the bakers to take their time getting used to it being there and seeing what it could do. I guess you might say the machine got used to the bakers, and was used extensively thereafter.

Other innovations in the culinary arts have continued to take place ever since those days, and will continue way into the future. Just remember that everything you think of as old was new at one time, and everything thought of as new today shall be older tomorrow. If you constantly look for better ways of doing everything you do every day, you will continue to be successful in your career for years to come.

Just think about the little things that you have today to work with, and think of the days before they were possible. For example, the prefilled icing tubes you can buy from your bakery supply house today and the smaller versions found in grocery stores in the baking section—can you remember when they were new? They were first introduced into the commercial market by H. A. Johnson in 1960 and into the retail market by McCormick's, the famous spice company based in Baltimore, Maryland, after purchasing Johnson and all its patents. They are most widely known by the name Cake Mate, and now come in many different types of icings, flavors, and colors.

I remember it well when they first hit the market, because I invented them. It was just an idea I had to make the work of decorating cakes and cookies a little easier. That's all, nothing grand or miraculous about it. You, too, might have an idea one day, and don't you dare be afraid to tell someone else. You never know when a simple idea can become a great thing.

Angel Food Cake
(48 servings)

Ingredients

2 lb.	Egg whites
	Vanilla (to taste)
1 lb.	Sugar
1/4 oz.	Cream of tartar
1/4 oz.	Salt
1 lb.	Sugar
13 oz.	Cake flour

Method

1. Beat egg whites and vanilla together about 5 min. at high speed.
2. Blend together sugar, cream of tartar, and salt. Add gradually to ingredients in Step 1. Beat.
3. Sift together sugar and cake flour. Add to the ingredients in Step 2 and fold in.

Scaling Instructions: Scale about 14 oz. to an 8 in. angel cake pan.
Baking Temperature: 350°F for 25 min.
Remarks: Precautions should be taken not to overbeat this mixture and to fold in Step 3 after it is thoroughly mixed. Otherwise the cake will collapse and the volume will be smaller. Turn the cake upside down after removing from the oven. Allow to cool before removing from the pan.

American Sponge Cake
(100 servings)

Ingredients

6 lb.	Sugar
4 lb., 8 oz.	Whole eggs
8 oz.	Egg yolks
	Vanilla or lemon extract (to taste)
1 oz.	Salt
2 lb., 8 oz.	Milk
8 oz.	Butter
4 lb., 8 oz.	Cake flour
2 oz.	Baking powder

Method

1. Place sugar in sheet pan and heat.
2. Add whole eggs, egg yolks, vanilla, and salt to sugar and beat to lemon color for about 10 min. at high speed.
3. Heat milk and butter together until butter is melted.
4. Sift together cake flour and baking powder and blend. Fold in with above alternately with milk. Mix as little as possible.

Baking Temperature: 375°F for 15 to 18 min.

Lady Fingers
(100 lady fingers)

Ingredients

1 lb.	Egg whites (16)
1 lb.	Sugar
	Vanilla (to taste)
10 oz.	Egg yolks (16)
1 lb.	Bread flour

Method

1. Whip egg whites. Add sugar gradually until a stiff meringue is made.
2. Whip egg yolks and add to stiff meringue. Fold in.
3. Sift bread flour and fold in.
4. Using a piping bag, pipe out 3 inch portions of dough. Space apart on the sheet pan to allow some spread.

Baking Temperature: 375°F–400°F for 7 to 8 min.

Joe and his wife Marge on their wedding day (1944).

An Apple Pie Sealed My Fate

On the morning of December 7, 1941 I was still working at Gilbert's Bakery alongside the other bakers who were busy pulling cake pans, cookies, and pastries out of the huge ovens when we heard President Franklin Delano Roosevelt interrupt the daily program with a very somber, yet inspiring speech. I remember everyone listening intently to what Roosevelt was saying, stopping their work in their tracks so they could hear every word. I will never forget it.

Earlier that morning the imperial forces of Japan attacked and bombed the American naval base in Pearl Harbor, Hawaii, killing thousands of young American sailors and civilians. America bombed? It was hard to imagine.

President Roosevelt had said it was every American's duty to come forward to help protect our country. He said we had no choice but to go to war, and that America needed us to defend its liberty. With every word he spoke I got more and more inflamed over the atrocity the Japanese had evoked, and was soon convinced that President Roosevelt was right. I agreed that we had no other choice but to stop what we were doing and join the service. The very next day (December 7th was a Sunday) I enlisted in the U.S. Army Air Corp, the forerunner of the U.S. Air Force, and was off on another great adventure.

Naively I assumed I would be placed in a cooking outfit because of my bakery experience and that I would continue the craft I had learned so well for over nine years. I was shocked to find myself assigned as an aircraft sheet metal specialist in the Mojave Desert. I was pretty good with flour and sugar, but what did I know about sheet metal, welding, or riveting? It was a necessary position at the time but one I knew nothing about.

It was still early in the war and there were only a few planes and fewer repairs needed at the air base in the desert. I was actually getting bored with my detail and wondered if I had made the right choice after all. I often found myself walking or standing near the mess hall (dining facility) in my spare time, which I had a lot of back then.

One day at mess I noticed the cooks serving small bowls filled with canned apples sprinkled with cinnamon and sugar for dessert. I was a little surprised to see that they had a good selection of basic ingredients, but had not put them together to form anything more elaborate than canned apples and seasonings in a shallow bowl. I thought to myself, *boy it would be nice to have a fresh-baked apple pie,* and it would give me something to do with all the spare time I had on my hands.

So I bravely asked the sergeant in charge of the mess hall why they didn't make pies out of the apples considering they did have sugar and cinnamon, and I was certain they had flour and fat to work with also. The sergeant, who was probably a sheet metal specialist himself in civilian life and knew nothing of cooking or baking, barked back that if they knew how to bake apple pies they would have done so. He then went on to say, sarcastically I think at first, that if I had nothing better to do I could come in and bake all the pies I wanted to. I wasn't sure if he was joking or giving me an order, but I quickly took up the idea and made plans to start baking the very next day.

As could be expected, the next day was just as uneventful as the previous few weeks, and I found myself walking over to the mess tent to see what mess (a more accurate use of the word) I could get into. It was easy to convince the cooks to let me help out, after all everyone likes a little help from time to time. So I found more canned apples, bags full of sugar and flour, and even some butter for the crust. Within a few minutes I was busy making apple pies and turnovers, to everyone's amazement.

Two days later I became the first in my battalion to be promoted to Private First Class (PFC) for outstanding service to my fellow soldiers and officers. I became a hero without even going to fight in the war. The soldiers honored me as much as they loved my pies.

One day a visiting general who had engine problems with one of the vehicles in his convoy stopped by the base for repairs. I was in the kitchen baking up a storm and didn't even know that he had made his way to the mess tent for a quick meal.

I was just pulling some of my pies out of the oven when one of the soldiers ran back into the kitchen and made the announcement that the general wanted something to eat. Generals in those days ate the same meals as the other soldiers, especially when traveling through remote places like the Mojave, and this meal was to be no exception. And just like all the other soldiers, when the general finished his meal he was served a hot piece of flaky apple pie, plain and naked on the plate but still steaming with hot juice and fresh flavor.

The next day the general sent for me, asking for me by name. He must have sent someone into the tent to see who was baking those pies the night before without my notice. Needless to say, I was quite nervous to be called to the officer's tent to meet with the general, not knowing why I had been called.

I was surprised at how friendly the general greeted me as soon as I walked in. Yes, I stood there at first in formal salute, but was quickly relaxed by the general's big smile and offer to shake my hand. You must know that officers, and particularly generals, do not ever show personal favoritism. In fact it was against all rules for them to do so; after all I was just another soldier doing his job for Uncle Sam. But he was so impressed that I had taken my own time, having learned already that I was not assigned as a baker, to take on the extra duty and bake the pies for the other soldiers' lunches and dinners that he had to meet Private Amendola face to face.

I guess he was impressed, not only with my baking, but more so with my willingness to do whatever it took to get the job done. Surely apple pies and turnovers were simple desserts, but for the general the act of baking them commanded great respect. In an instant the general had already made up his mind that he wanted me to join his outfit and help spread more goodwill and good food throughout the army.

A dispute quickly ensued between the general and my commanding officer at the time, who didn't want to lose his star pastry chef/sheet metal specialist to the battlegrounds of Europe. Besides, it went against army protocol to select a single soldier out of all the ranks of eligible men for this kind of assignment. After all, there were rules that had to be followed and discipline among all the soldiers that had to be maintained.

I'm not really sure what happened next, but within a few weeks after the general left the base I found myself promoted once again, this time to corporal, and transferred to London, England. There I was assigned to the officer's headquarters where not just one, but many generals, colonels, and other officers in both armies (U.S. and Great Britain) tried to steal a few minutes away from the war to enjoy a good, wholesome meal. So I guess you might say that the apple pie the general ate, as humble a dessert as it was, sealed my fate and gave me the first real promotion in military rank and life itself.

I made the crossing from New York to Scotland on the refurbished *Queen Mary*, which was commissioned by the army as a wartime transport. "Gray Ghost" was the nickname given the *Queen Mary*, for it was so fast on the seas it seemed to appear, disappear, and appear again out of the enemy's reach. Over 15,000 troops (five times the *Queen Mary's* normal accompaniment of guests) sailed at one time on its decks and in its quarters. There were so many of us on board that we took turns sleeping, having to share our cots with three or four other people. But I'll leave the *Queen Mary* story for another chapter.

From Scotland we drove in trucks and jeeps down to London, England, where we would be headquartered. It was in London that I met the young and beautiful Marjorie Meatyard, whom I persuaded to marry me with my charm, my courtesy and, I truly believe, my ability to bake. She's been by my side now for over fifty-eight years, canvassing the world as we build a great life together.

It was also during my London experience that I was able to take a leave to go visit my Grandmother Lucibello who was still living in Amalfi, Italy, a small fishing town on the east coast of the Mediterranean Sea, with many of my aunts and uncles whom I had never seen before.

It was great staying in the remote town, which was yet untouched by the war ravaging around it. I even tried to put the war behind me when resting on the calm Italian beaches, but I knew my place was back in London doing what I did best.

When it was time to go back to London my Grandmother gave me a small box of chocolate truffles (round chocolate candies coated with rich chocolate ganache) and their secret recipe. That same recipe is still with me today, and I'm now preparing to launch a whole new line of Amalfi Chocolates™. The journey continues . . .

I was stationed to the Cumberland Hotel in London for most of the war. There was a very famous band leader and his ensemble who had also enlisted in the Army Air Corps and were stationed at the Cumberland while I was there. It was the popular Alton Glenn Miller, who had joined the Air Corps in 1942 determined to entertain troops in war with the music he had developed over his short lifetime. Some of his existing band members joined with him, but once in the service it didn't take Miller long to put together the Glenn Miller Army Air Force Band, which would entertain nearly 600,000 troops during their tenure in the military.

Unfortunately, Miller would be lost in the war while traveling in a transport plane from London to Paris in 1944. He was headed there to make arrangements for a Christmas musical festival before sending for his band to follow. His plane was lost, either shot down by planes or due to engine trouble; no one will ever know; Miller was never heard from again.

It wasn't until after V.E. Day (Victory in Europe Day, May 8, 1945) that I was assigned to the Hotel Plaza Athena in Paris. This hotel was also used primarily for senior officers now stationed in the French capital: Lt. colonels, colonels, and generals were our guests.

The executive chef in charge at that time was Lucian Diat, brother of the famous chef Louis Diat who was also a food writer for gourmet magazines. Both Diat brothers had worked with Escoffier, and were well entrenched in his teachings. I was one of the three GIs assigned to this kitchen at the hotel, and what a great experience it was.

I will never forget the lessons I learned, both in baking and in dealing with people. If I had just stood back and did nothing, like the rest of the soldiers in the Mojave assignment, I would never have had the opportunities I had. Who knows, but I might have ended up in battle instead of in two world-famous hotels baking desserts for some of the world's most powerful military officers and politicians. While it's definitely true that I was not out of danger, I heard many bombs drop over London when stationed there, I was somewhat secure in my position, working with baking pans and ovens instead of rifles and tanks.

If you wait for opportunities they may never come; sometimes you have to make your own opportunities happen.

Apple Strudel Dough
(25 servings)

Ingredients

5 lb.	Bread flour
3 lb.	Pastry flour
1/8 lb.	Salt
1	Egg
1/4 lb.	Shortening
4 lb. (2 qts.)	Water

Method

1. Mix all ingredients into a smooth dough. Shape into a ball and brush with vegetable oil. Let dough relax for 1/2 hr. Spread dough on a 36 in. by 36 in. cloth and stretch until thin and transparent. This dough will make a 30 in. by 30 in. square.
2. Brush entire surface with butter; egg wash bottom.
3. Spread filling leaving 2 in. on each side. Fold ends under. Roll like jelly roll. Cut in half and place on paper-lined pan. Brush with butter.

Baking Temperature: 400°F for 45 min.

Apple Filling for Strudel
(25 servings)

Ingredients

8 oz.	Butter
7 lb.	Apples, No. 10 can
1 lb.	Brown sugar
1 tsp.	Cinnamon
8 oz.	Raisins
12 oz.	Cake, cubed or diced, toasted

Method

1. Melt butter. Add remaining ingredients. Bring to a simmer. Remove from heat.
2. Add cubed or diced toasted cake to ingredients in Step 1.

Remarks: Use with rolled-out strudel dough.

Chocolate Shavings or Curls

Ingredients

Chocolate coating

Method

1. Melt to approximately 100°F. Cool to 85°F.
2. Spread out on tray or marble slab. Continue cooling until chocolate becomes firm.
3. Using a small pastry cutter or spatula, scrape chocolate into shavings or curls.

Remarks: Chocolate shavings and curls make a very effective garnish for pies, cakes, ice cream, etc.

For Chocolate Curls: Follow Step 1 above. Then spread a thin coating of the chocolate, about 5 or 6 in. wide, on a marble slab. When this cools and sets, lightly rub top of chocolate with the palm of the hand. Hold a french knife at 45-degree angle and cut in 1 in. strips, pushing up and forward so chocolate curls.

Éclair and Cream Puff Paste Desserts

Ingredients

2 lb.	Water or milk
1 lb.	Shortening or butter
1/2 oz.	Salt
1 lb., 8 oz.	Bread flour
2 lb., 8 oz.	Eggs (variable—about 24)

Method

1. Bring water or milk and shortening or butter and salt mixed together to a good rolling boil.
2. Combine bread flour with Step 1. Blend. Cook over medium heat until the mixture is smooth and rolls free from side of pot. Remove from heat.
3. Add eggs slowly until a medium-stiff paste is obtained. Blend well after each addition of eggs.

Baking Temperature: 400°F for 30 min.

Precautions:
1. Make sure that the shortening and water are brought to a good rolling boil.
2. Be sure shortening is melted.
3. Mixture in Step 2 should be dry when cooked and not stick to pot.
4. Consistency of mix is very important. Common mistakes are using too many eggs or using too few eggs.
5. Incorrect addition of eggs must be avoided (add only 2 or 3 at a time, blending in well after each addition).
6. Shell must not be removed from oven until it is completely dry or it will collapse.

Polka Tart

1. Roll out pie crust or pastry dough about 1/8 in. thick. Cut a circle about 8 in. in diameter for a large tart, 3 in. in diameter for an individual tart.
2. Place dough on a baking sheet lined with baking paper. Using a plain tube, dress out a rim of cream puff paste around the edge.
3. Bake at 400°F for about 30 min. or until golden brown. Cool; fill with pastry cream.
4. Place a generous amount of granulated sugar on top of pastry cream. Caramelize the sugar by pressing a red-hot poker on top of the pastry.

Reader's Notes and Thoughts

RMS Queen Mary known as the Gray Ghost.

RMS Queen Mary: The Gray Ghost

The outbreak of World War II greatly affected the way the world conducted business. Everything was changed the day Hitler invaded
Poland in 1939, although it took the world a few more years of Nazi
buildup to admit it was at war.

Manufacturing industries would soon switch from making appli-
ances to airplanes and bombs; the auto industry would change from
sedans and coupes to tanks, jeeps, and other land transports; even pen-
nies would one day be made out of lead because all the copper was being
used in ammunition. Whatever we thought of as normal had changed;
sometimes for the better and sometimes never to be the same again.

It wasn't long before trains and cruise ships were also recruited for
military service. My first trip to London was aboard the *Queen Mary*. Yes,
the famous *Queen Mary*, sister ship to *Queen Elizabeth*, two of the world's
largest and fastest cruise ships at the time, both of which traded rich and
influential passengers for troops, medics, guns, and ammunition.

No ocean, sky, or land was safe from Hitler's far-reaching armies, especially after Italy and then Japan joined his side. It would take courage,
strength, resolve, and ingenuity for the rest of the world to be able to es-
cape the combined strength of their armies, navies, and air power.

Then on the fated December 7th in 1941 when America was finally
drawn into the war, my whole life changed when I turned in my rolling
pin for a rifle. From that moment onward the world would be different;
win or loose, America was going to war, and I was going along.

The *Queen Mary* was the first vessel launched after the merger of Cu-
nard and White Star Steamship Companies, two of the United Kingdom's
largest steamship builders, in 1934. She was the largest and fastest ocean
vessel when she left dry dock in Clydebank, Scotland on September 26th
of the same year. She could carry upwards of 2,300 passengers and crew
in luxurious accommodations, almost twice as many as the other leading
cruise ships of the time, and at twice the speed. A typical cross-Atlantic
voyage would take two to three weeks; the *Queen Mary* effortlessly sailed
the ocean in just under six days.

Before America was drawn into the war the *Queen Mary* had already
been enlisted to carry troops to other parts of the world needing support
and defense from the outreaching Third Reich. Troops were desperately

needed to strengthen the defenses of Britain, Australia, and New Zealand, and to halt the erosion of Allied strongholds in the Middle and Far East; getting them there proved to be a monumental task.

Once enlisted in military service the *Queen Mary* was rechristened as the "Gray Ghost," for she seemed to appear and disappear quickly on the open seas, undetectable by German u-boats and battle ships.

By the winter of 1942 the escalation in the war required even more soldiers, arms, and vehicles than the passenger ships could provide given their luxurious accommodations and grand dining halls. Yet, under order of the British government, on January 24, 1942 the *Queen Mary* entered dry dock in Boston's naval yard to be transformed from a luxury cruise liner to a war transport ship. Her new design would enable her to carry 9,000 troops and crew across the seas, practically three times her original capacity.

I believe it was the Bethlehem Steel Company in Pennsylvania that supplied all the steel for the extra bunks. Thousands of bunks and narrow steel-framed beds would soon fill her hull and line the sides of the decks where dance floors and lounges once stood. This would be the first of two major renovations the *Queen Mary* would undergo during her military service.

The struggle against Germany and Italy had also reached a turning point by the spring of 1943, and the myth of Hitler's invincibility had already begun to fade after successful Allied victories in North Africa and Russia. The Allies had faced the best that Germany, Italy, and Japan could offer, and had survived.

When Italy finally fell in October of 1943 it set up the stage for a full invasion against France and then Germany itself, the last two remaining strongholds of the German army in Europe. But before any such assault could be mounted the men and equipment necessary to guarantee victory had to be shipped to the battle zone.

The speed and passenger capacity of the *Queen Mary* and the *Queen Elizabeth*, her sister ship, made them the obvious choices to lead in the offensive. Yet they were still only capable of housing just under 9,000 troops each, after one refitting in dry dock a year earlier, which was not nearly enough to feed the great number of troops necessary for a decisive assault.

Once again the *Queen Mary* was refitted, this time with nearly 12,000 bunks, while resting in New York Harbor in May of 1943. The amount of troops she would carry caused some worry to the engineers involved. Should all the men stand on one side of the ship at the same time, they theorized, the ship could list dangerously and possibly sink. So they went about designing a plan that would prevent this kind of accident.

To reduce the risk that this might happen, the ship was divided into three vertical and completely segregated troop accommodation areas, designated Red, White, and Blue, and once you were assigned to one you were never to enter another for fear of being placed in on-board detention. We were given colored buttons corresponding to our assigned area, and were warned of the grave danger our sheer mass would place us in if we didn't follow strict directions. The coloring system was also how we were going to share accommodations and meals, by zone colors and by times in the day.

We began boarding the liner on the afternoon of July 22, 1943, one day before her scheduled departure. Each one of us was expected to carry our own M-1 rifle, helmet, canteen, cartridge belts, and a full field pack, as well as two bags containing complete summer and winter uniforms and whatever personal belongings could be squeezed into the full pack. I can remember the Red Cross workers passing out coffee and donuts as we assembled in the boarding area, waiting in long lines while a military band played music and popular dance tunes. The doughnuts were okay, but I did long for the smells of the bakeshop I had left two years earlier.

Finally, with troops, crew, fuel, and provisions aboard, the *Queen Mary* was ready for sea. Departures were usually made either early in the morning or late in the evening, both to catch the maximum high tide and to screen the liner's movement from view. Once the liner crossed over the Hudson Tunnel the harbor pilot disembarked by launch and the *Queen Mary* made her way to the open sea.

Life for the troops on the *Queen Mary* was controlled by the ship's Standing Orders and by the routine Daily Orders published and distributed by the crew. The Standing Orders covered such things as emergency procedures for air attack and the outbreak of fire, as well as security precautions regarding life at sea in wartime. The Daily Orders, on the other hand, dealt with the more mundane matters of work assignments, religious services, and the myriad of details necessary to keep 15,000 men fed and entertained for six days.

Two meals were served aboard the *Queen Mary* each day, each in six different sittings, with breakfast available from 6:30 to 11:00 AM and dinner from 3:00 to 7:00 PM. The enlisted men were fed in the former first-class dining room, and the Officer's Mess was the former tourist lounge. Meal times were usually scenes of controlled chaos, for each sitting was allowed only 45 minutes to enter, eat, and make room for the next group. The rooms were filled with cigarette smoke, the banging of mess kits and silverware, and the sound of thousands of men waiting noisily in line for their turns at the tables. At the end of each sitting one group of soldiers would be coming in as the previous group was being ushered out the opposite end of the dining hall.

The rotational system of scheduling meals on the *Queen Mary* was also applied to sleeping arrangements. Only two-thirds of the troops could be accommodated in the liner's newly fitted 12,500 standee bunks, leaving 2,500 men assigned to sleeping areas on the ship's decks. A regular rotation ensured that no one spent more than two nights "topside," though many of the GIs actually preferred it to the crowded spaces below. The bunks had been stacked six high in every available area, and were usually separated by only 18 inches between them.

The fear of a German attack was ever-present among the troops, and the daily practice firings of the *Queen Mary's* weapons were conducted as much for morale purposes as for gunnery training. These drills were always popular with the troops, both as a reassuring demonstration of the ship's ability to defend herself and as a form of welcome, if rather noisy, entertainment, and were often the high point of an otherwise boring day at sea.

Once safely moored alongside her pier in Gourock, Scotland exactly six days later, we left the *Queen Mary* and were transported by truck to the various parts of Scotland and England where we would be stationed. Gangways on multiple decks were used to off-load the troops, and the debarkation process took nearly thirty-six hours.

The voyage I was on was the first time that any sea-going vessel carried more than 15,000 people on board. The *Queen Mary* kept up its hectic schedule from June 1943 to April 1945, and during that period sailed over 180,000 miles and carried nearly 340,000 American and Canadian servicemen to the United Kingdom. The *Queen Elizabeth* was working equally hard. The two great ships transported the majority of men ordered to battle in Great Britain during Operation Bolero.

Puff Paste Desserts
(about 100)

Ingredients

5 lb.	Bread flour
1 oz.	Salt
8 oz.	Butter
8 oz.	Eggs (5)
2 lb. (2 pints)	Cold water
5 lb.	Butter or puff paste shortening

Method

1. Mix together flour, salt, butter, eggs, and cold water into a dough. Remove from mixer. Round into a ball shape. Allow to stand 15 to 20 min.
2. Roll Step 1 into Step 2. Directions for this process are given below.

Baking Temperature: 350°F–375°F for 20 to 25 min.

Precautions:
1. Roll the dough following the direction of the four corners. Leave the center somewhat thicker.
2. Place shortening in center and lap over the four sides.
3. Roll out again about 1/2 in. thick and twice as long as it is wide.
4. After brushing off all excess flour, fold both ends toward middle and then double again.
5. Allow the dough to stand in a cool place or put in the refrigerator for at least 20 to 30 min.
6. Repeat the rolling process four times. On the final roll, make a "three-way fold."

Cheese Sticks
1. Give two turns to a 1 lb. piece of puff paste. Dust between folds with 2 oz. grated cheese mixed with salt and paprika.
2. Roll out to about 1/6 in. thick into strips 1 in. wide.
3. Roll these strips into twisted sticks. Place on wet sheet pans. Allow to stand 30 min.
4. Bake at 375°F for 20 to 25 min. After baking, cut into strips of 4 in. lengths. Serve.

Fancy Butter Cookies (Spritz)
(24 dozen cookies)

Ingredients

8 oz.	Almond paste
1 lb, 8 oz.	Confectioner's sugar
1 lb.	Eggs
2 lb.	Shortening and butter
3 lb.	Cake flour

Method

1. Rub together almond paste and sugar.
2. Add eggs gradually to obtain a smooth batter.
3. Add shortening and butter and whip until light.
4. Add cake flour and mix until smooth. Do not overmix.
5. Using a piping bag, pipe out to form various shapes.

Baking Temperature: 375°F for about 10 to 12 min.

Charlottes

Charlotte Russe
1. Trim the required number of lady fingers and line the bottom of a plain Charlotte mold with the lady fingers.
2. Line the sides of the mold with lady fingers.
3. Place bavarian cream mixture in the center of the mold. Allow to set in refrigerator.
4. Unmold on a cold dish and decorate with whipped cream. (Charlotte Russe can also be prepared in individual molds or portions.)

Charlotte Royale
1. Line a round bowl with sliced jelly rolls.
2. Fill with bavarian cream mixture.
3. Chill in refrigerator.
4. Unmold and decorate with whipped cream.

Strawberry Charlotte
1. Line the bottom of a plain Charlotte mold with strawberry jelly.
2. Line the sides with lady fingers.
3. Fill the center with a strawberry bavarian cream mixture.
4. When set, unmold the Charlotte on a cold dish and decorate or garnish with whipped cream and strawberries.

Note: Peach, raspberry, apricot, or any other fruit can be used in place of strawberry to make a fruit-flavored Charlotte.

Original building of the Culinary Institute of America 393 Prospect St. New Haven, CT.

393 Prospect Street

M Charles Rovetti was manager of the Aschenbrodel Restaurant in New Haven Connecticut in 1943 when Edward Rahm (another New Haven restaurant owner) and Richard H. Dargan, an official of the New Haven Dairy Association, joined forces to launch the New Haven Restaurant Association. Both men, as well as Rovetti and every other restaurateur in New Haven, had growing concerns over the shortage of trained culinarians for back-of-the-house operations and the lack of professional front-of-the-house waiters, waitresses, and managers that the growing industry was suffering. The Restaurant Association seemed to be the best idea they could come up with to join forces, thoughts, energy, and funds to work on the labor shortage we all faced.

It was World War II, begun in 1941, which had drained New Haven of its professional cook and waiter hopefuls and many practiced professionals as well, all of whom had given up their knives and spatulas for guns and ammunition. But it was a two-edged sword. Not only did American men and women join the service to protect their country, but foreign cooks, bakers, maitre d's, and chefs also halted their normal immigration to the United States under the cloud of global war. Within a brief two years, every dining facility in New Haven operated with short staffs, and some closed their doors forever for a lack of professionals to run their kitchens, bakeries, and dining rooms.

It was in July of 1943 that Charles Rovetti resigned his post at the Aschenbrodel Restaurant to take on the full-time position of executive secretary for the newly formed New Haven Restaurant Association, with Richard Dargan as its first president. Their first agenda item was how to save the New Haven restaurant industry from collapsing due to a lack of trained workers for their staffs.

Almost immediately, Dargan and Rovetti petitioned William Cronin, then the head of the War Manpower Commission in Connecticut, to help them save the industry by placing a blockade on the recruitment of culinary and other restaurant professionals into the service. It was an unusual request, considering that the scope of the war effort affected everything from manpower to manufactured goods (most American industries switched from making washing machines and refrigerators to tanks, rifles, and mortar shells), but one which they felt was necessary in order to keep the restaurants, bakeries, and hotels open.

In September 1943, through the efforts of Cronin, the restaurant industry in New Haven and throughout Connecticut was declared an essential industry, thus halting the draft of its men and women into military service. It was a milestone achievement for the newly formed Restaurant Association, but it was only the first step.

The New Haven Restaurant Association soon grew to over three hundred members, including fifty wholesalers and suppliers as associate members. Dargan and Rovetti were still its only stalwart officers and began to build relationships, both professional and personal, with other restaurant associations in nearby states and around the country.

It seemed that everywhere they traveled and everyone they talked to had the same grave concerns over the availability of trained professionals for America's restaurants and hotels, the greatest shortage being in the back-of-the-house because of the specialized training it takes to run kitchens and bakeries. Something had to be done to alleviate those concerns then and in the future, or the restaurant industry would continue to suffer great losses and closures.

Less than two years later, in 1945, Dargan and Rovetti began the search for a location for what they envisioned would become a vital school for the training of much needed restaurant professionals. One location, a building on the corner of Fair and State Streets in New Haven, was up for lease, and it was soon thereafter that the New Haven Restaurant Institute was born.

Obtaining the building was only the first step of the process. The second, and perhaps hardest step, was to raise the needed funds to equip the new school and hire the administration and teachers to run it. With the aid of the Association's clerical secretary, Anna Smith, Harry Legelis, the Association's treasurer, Dargan and Rovetti set about designing a campaign to raise the needed funds from the Association membership. After much hard work and inspired pleas, $200 donations started coming into the Association's coffers for the establishment and operation of the needed school. The initial amount raised was a mere $12,700, but it was enough to get started in earnest with the plans to create and operate the Institute.

Frances L. Roth was a New Haven attorney with many political and social ties throughout the region when she was approached by Dargan to become the Institute's first administrative director. It was Dargan's hope that her energy, personality, and connections would be the magic the Institute needed to raise the even greater amount of funds and other donations the Institute would need in order to train young people for careers in the restaurant industry. Operating a restaurant school was and still is an extremely expense proposition, and the seed money that was raised from the Association's membership was just enough to secure the location and Mrs. Roth's services.

The hiring of Mrs. Roth was the best thing that could have happened, for she quickly and eagerly took on the challenge of courting food and equipment manufacturers and suppliers from all over New England to help the Institute open its doors. With persuasive insistence and her personal charm Mrs. Roth was extremely successful at asking for money and procuring the food and equipment necessary to help train the future cooks, bakers, and chefs that were so badly needed.

The selection of the Institute's faculty was the next step in its progression from idea to reality. But who would be selected to begin the process of interviewing and training faculty for the kitchen and dining room classrooms that were already being designed and built? Just a few months before the Institute was supposed to register its first class of students, retired U.S. Army Lieutenant Carroll Dooley was hired as the chairman of the division of food and food preparation of the New Haven Restaurant Institute because of his extensive background in all phases of food production and restaurant management, prior to his enlistment in the Army and continued throughout his tour of duty, and his military stature and contacts.

Finally, after much hard work and dedication, the New Haven Restaurant Institute opened its classroom doors for the first time on May 22, 1946, with eighteen students and only two faculty members.

Mrs. Roth was also a close friend of the then-president of Yale University and his wife, Mr. and Mrs. Roland Angell (Katharine Angell), who followed the development of the new school and its fast expansion. It was soon obvious to everyone connected to the Institute that the storefront building on First Street was not going to offer enough space for the continued growth of the school, and additional space would have to be secured.

Joe Amendola with Katharine Angell.

Through some funding and political ties, Mrs. Angell helped Mrs. Roth identify and purchase an old carriage house and garage on the edge of Yale's expansive property at 393 Prospect Street, which was quickly converted to more classrooms and offices for expanding student enrollment, faculty, and administration.

Enrollment grew so quickly that the New Haven Restaurant Association, which had been sharing office space on the second floor of the building, had to relocate to another site so that additional classrooms could be built. By March of 1947 the Institute became fully self-sufficient and no longer needed the support of time and money from the Restaurant Association, and in fact had already repaid most of the borrowed money that was put up just two years earlier to finance the operation.

The Institute continued to grow and expand and by 1948 it had already started a baking program in tangent with the already successful cooking program. Needless to say, the Institute needed to hire more baking instructors for both the cooking and the new baking curriculum.

I can remember driving up to the New Haven Restaurant Institute's administrative offices on 393 Prospect St. in my newly acquired 1939 Nash-Lafitte coupe. I was a trained baker just returned from my extended tour of duty with international training and exposure, and thought I could contribute the knowledge and skills I had obtained to other GIs needing to learn a trade after they put away their guns and tanks. Practically all of the students of the Institute at that time were sponsored by the G.I. Bill of Rights, and with my military background I knew I had the skills and knowledge required to speak on their level yet bring them up to the level of professional cook and/or baker.

I was first interviewed by Harry Herman, who was the food director at that time, and was surprised when he told me that I was too young to be a baking or pastry chef instructor. Even with my experience supervising those twenty-nine German bakers at Gilbert's and my extensive military career in London and Paris, Herman was afraid I would not be successful training the GIs, many of whom were older than I was.

I didn't accept the no answer from Herman even though I knew his position and his opinion would weigh heavily on anyone else I would speak to. But I insisted on speaking directly to Mrs. Roth, who, I had heard, had actually started the school basically out of nothing. Surely she would understand the value of my experience, but also my tenacity on not walking away at the first no answer.

As could be expected, Mrs. Roth echoed Mr. Herman's decision that I was too young to be able to teach older GIs the principles and techniques that were needed for the baking and pastry program. Through perseverance I persuaded her that I would be a very good baking and pastry instructor, already having over eighteen years of extensive experience including my time at the Cumberland Hotel in London and the Hotel

Plaza Athena in Paris. I suppose when I mentioned that I had worked with Chef Diat in Paris that she finally decided to give me a try. However, she would only agree to hire me on a part-time basis to see how the students would react to me being just twenty-seven years old at that time.

My part-time position at the Institute only lasted for one week, for when Mrs. Roth and Mr. Herman saw my craftsmanship and teaching ability they were immediately impressed and offered me a full-time position right in the bakeshop I was teaching in.

Ironically, that part-time job I was offered lasted for forty-one years—until 1988 when I resigned. My career with the now-titled Culinary Institute of America (CIA) included:

- Baking and Pastry Instructor (1947–1965)
- Assistant Dean of Students (1965–1971)
- Dean of Student Affairs (in Hyde Park, 1971–1975)
- Vice President of Student Affairs (1975–1978)
- Interim President (1978–1979)
- Senior Vice President (1979–1988)

After spending a lifetime of teaching, baking, and pastry and holding various administrative positions at the Culinary Institute of America for over 40 years, I remain active as ambassador of CIA for the rest of my life.

Nougat

Ingredients

1 lb.	Sugar
1/4 oz.	Lemon
12 oz.	Almonds (sliced)

Method

1. Combine sugar and lemon and cook on moderate heat until golden brown.
2. Remove from heat. Combine almonds with Step 1.
3. Spread mixture on an oiled marble slab. Roll out with lightly oiled rolling pin and cut with a lightly oiled knife to desired shapes. Allow to cool and harden.

Baking Temperature: 250°F (for as long as needed).
Remarks: To hold pieces of nougat in place, use caramelized sugar. First dip the pieces in it, then put them in place and hold them in position until set. After all pieces of the desired decoration have been assembled, add small dots of royal icing.

Fruit Conde
(15 servings)

Ingredients

1 pt.	Milk
1 lb.	Blanched rice
1/4 oz.	Salt
4 oz.	Sugar
1/2 oz.	Gelatin, unflavored
1 pt.	Heavy cream, whipped
6 oz.	Nesselrode mixture (canned fruit)

Method

1. Place milk, rice, salt, sugar, and gelatin in a pot and simmer for about 10 min. Allow to cool and set.
2. Whip cream and fold into mixture that has been set (Step 1). Add nesselrode mixture. Place this mixture in a large or small Charlotte mold. Refrigerate until mixture is set.
3. When set, unmold on a dish; place assorted fruit on top of rice mixture. Brush top of fruit with a hot apricot sauce and serve.

Torte De Riccota (Torte of Italian Cheese)
(8 to 10 servings—1 pie or cake)

Ingredients

1 lb., 8 oz.	Riccotta
4 oz.	Sugar
1/8 oz.	Salt
1 oz.	Vanilla (to taste)
1 oz.	Citron (diced fine)
4	Eggs
1 oz.	Brandy
4 oz.	Toasted almonds

Method

1. Rub riccotta and mix with sugar through fine sieve.
2. Mix salt, vanilla, and citron; add to ingredients in Step 1.
3. Add eggs gradually to ingredients above.
4. Make pie dough for bottom and top. Make lattice top by cutting dough in strips and weaving them together.
5. Dust with confectioner's sugar.

Baking Temperature: 350°F for about 45 min.

Reader's Notes and Thoughts

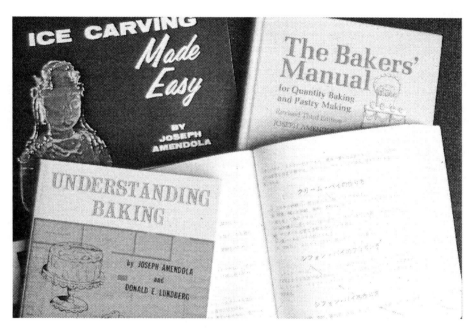

Covers of Joe Amendola's books—*Ice Carving Made Easy, The Baker's Manual,* and *Understanding Baking.*

Publishing Door to Door

By 1960, I had been an instructor at the Culinary Institute of America for over twelve years and had to develop all of my own baking notes and recipes for the students to use in class from the beginning. There was nothing else.

Over the years, beginning with my apprenticeship with my uncle, then moving on to Gilbert's Bakery as production supervisor, and capped off by my experiences in London and Paris, baking and collecting recipes all the time, I had amassed quite an encyclopedia of notes, techniques, and step-by-step recipes that had been tested hundreds if not thousands of times each. Then, through many years of teaching at the Institute, I was forced to create my own lecture notes to accompany the recipes in order to teach baking to people who didn't know the difference between quick breads and rolls, cake flour and bread flour, or icings and sweetened shortenings.

I went about categorizing all the knowledge I had acquired and breaking it down into very minute pieces that could be taught to a class of students one lesson at a time. I have always believed it is better to learn how to bake rather than learning a hundred or more baking recipes, because once you understand the theories and science behind baking it is easier to make a whole array of bakery products with consistent results.

Just following recipes was not enough for students to learn from; they needed in-depth study tools and controlled practice in the bakeshop in order to gain proficiency. After all, the whole purpose of the Institute was to train returning GIs in a new craft in the short time they would be at the Institute compared to what they could have learned, as I did, after many years as an apprentice and bakery worker working their way up the career ladder one pastry at a time.

I credit the CIA and Mrs. Roth personally for inspiring me to publish my notes and recipes as the *Baker's Manual* in 1960. Mrs. Roth and I had many conversations about teaching and learning, and she felt, as I do, that there is a four-step phase to learning a new craft: seeing, hearing, studying, and doing. In other words, students learn by watching someone else perform a task or produce a recipe, by listening to the teacher explain all the steps and procedures as they work, by studying notes and recipes, and by repeating the steps themselves in a supervised environment where they can get immediate feedback.

The lecture and laboratory setup at the Culinary Institute was perfect for developing culinary skill, but what notes would the students have to study by at night other than those they managed to write themselves during the day? Even in the best of circumstances where the students got a lot of recipes and notes to copy down, each class was only as good as the experiences and knowledge the teachers managed to collect throughout their lives. Given a knowledgeable and experienced baker and pastry chef, the class would be credible; given a teacher with limited skills and knowledge, learning would become harder to ensure and difficult to measure. As a result, when the students would move from class to class they may or may not have had the prerequisite skills and knowledge necessary for the new lessons.

Without solid teaching guides, notes, and tested recipes the students would be at the whim of their instructors' personal preferences and experiences. If a teacher were more proficient in cookies and pies, that's all the students would learn; if a teacher were proficient in European desserts, then those would be the lessons the students would learn and practice. Unfortunately it would also mean that no matter how willing the instructor was to share his or her knowledge, and no matter how hard the students studied and practiced their skills, results would be inconsistent at best. Some students would become proficient in the same knowledge and skills, but would they have the variety of knowledge and skills needed to make them successful in baking and pastry positions in the foodservice industry?

It wasn't so important in the early years at the New Haven Restaurant Institute to have a structured curriculum because there were only a few instructors who shared their notes and expertise with the other instructors in close concert with each other. This firm yet open-ended teaching model worked well for many years. However, once the Institute opened its doors to students other than GIs and increased its curriculum to cover various aspects of cooking and baking, having an established curriculum covering very specific knowledge and skills became paramount to the success of the Institute and the ability of graduates to find gainful employment.

It's hard to imagine today, where there is a new culinary textbook published practically every day, but in the 1950s and early 1960s there were none. Of course we had the old classic references like Escoffier's *Le Guide Culinaire* (1912) and Ranhofer's *The Epicurean* (1894), but as good as those books were in standardizing and referencing menu items and listing their ingredients and procedures, they did little to teach beginning culinarians the theories and science of cooking and baking that it would take to prepare the recipes they chronicled. The students Escoffier and Ranhofer addressed their recipes toward would have already obtained a high level of knowledge and skill in the culinary arts; in our case we had to assume the students knew nothing, or very little about culinary arts.

Novice students need to start from the beginning and learn everything they can about the craft. For baking and pastry students, and culinary students learning baking, this meant a thorough introduction to the ingredients, methods, and science of baking was needed before recipes and formulas were ever discussed.

I knew that students needed study guides and reference books if they were ever going to be able to learn the huge amounts of information that the baking and culinary profession required for its craft. Sure, we could produce various bakery items every day, until the students knew them inside and out, but what would they have really learned about baking? All they would learn is how to follow directions, and bakery managers and chefs need a lot more than that to succeed.

Mrs. Roth finally convinced me to publish my own set of notes and recipes for the students to use. No one else, she felt, had as accurate a record of detailed notes and procedures on baking and recipes that had already been tested time and time again. After all, I had been working there over twelve years by then, and I guess had formed some king of reputation for being thorough and accurate. I always strived to teach at the students' level without talking down to them, and never hesitated going over the information again and again until they got it. Everything I had for class notes, then, was already broken down into the minutest detail. All I had to do was reorganize the information into chapters and paragraphs, and the beginning of the *Baker's Manual* was on its way.

We didn't have the slew of big publishing houses like Prentice Hall, John Wiley & Sons, and McGraw-Hill pounding the pavement for culinary textbooks back then. After all, who would use them besides the students at the Institute? Neither were there the hundreds of culinary colleges that we have today. So even for the most progressive thinker, what possibly could the prospective book sales look like outside of New Haven, Connecticut?

As Mrs. Roth and I searched practically door to door through many New York publishing houses and received rejection after rejection, we might have felt defeated, but instead we felt even more determined to make the book a reality. Every time we returned to the Institute and faced the growing number of students entering the foodservice industry who needed such a book, we were encouraged to keep trying.

Finally, on a subsequent trip to New York City we happened upon a small publishing company, Ahrens Publishing on South Park Avenue, which had already published a couple of successful hospitality books and gave us an appointment to pitch our project. Mrs. Roth and I entered the room together, but it was she who put her attorney-like deliberation skills to work, once again pleading the case for a textbook dedicated to baking science. It was invigorating to watch Mrs. Roth in action. By the time we left the meeting I had the feeling they wouldn't dare turn down this persuasive woman, or risk her coming back again with even more veracity.

I must have been right, because within a few days we received a letter saying they would publish the *Baker's Manual* (1958) in its entirety. It was late 1957, and by spring of the next year my book was being used for the first time by cooking and baking students at the Institute. The fourth edition of the book was published by John Wiley & Sons in 1993, and it is still selling world wide. Translations of the *Baker's Manual* appear in both Japanese and Chinese, and all because of personal and business contacts that I had made.

The quick success of the book encouraged both Mrs. Roth and me to write and publish a second book on baking. This time I would take the approach that I spoke of earlier: presenting the basic theories and science of baking in terms beginning students and practicing culinarians (bakers) could understand.

I happened to get a copy of a new book, at that time, called *Understanding Cooking*, by Don Lundberg, a professor in the hospitality management department at the University of Massachusetts. I was so impressed with the ease of the prose yet the depth of the information that I called Professor Lundberg at the University and asked if he would meet with me to discuss the new book project I was dreaming up.

The Institute had already begun to gain a reputation as a fine school, and my *Baker's Manual* had quickly earned a reputation for accuracy and clarity. So when I called Lundberg he actually took my call.

I told him over the phone how much I loved his new book, and that I would consider it a great honor if he would meet me one day for lunch or dinner. He accepted my invitation and I found myself driving to the University the next day.

We hit it off immediately and were quickly consumed in conversation about the subject and treatment I had envisioned for this next baking book. I told him we were all very happy with the *Baker's Manual*, but that the students needed more information, and particularly more information on the theories and science of baking.

When I told him it was his book, *Understanding Cooking*, that inspired me to write the second book, although I had already made plans to do so before I read his, I had won his friendship forever. Apparently he had wanted to do a baking companion to his book, but didn't have the breadth of information that was needed to do a good job by himself. By making that phone call that fortuitous day I had answered a prayer he prayed in quiet, and he mine when he accepted my invitation, both of us without even knowing either prayer existed.

Within a year, *Understanding Baking*, co-authored by Joe Amendola and Don Lundberg, was published by Ahrens Publishing Company in 1960.

Don and I remained friends until his death many years later.

My next book had nothing to do with baking at all (*Ice Carving Made Easy*), but that is an entire story by itself, which I shall tell in the next chapter.

I also wrote another baking book, *Professional Baking*, in 1965, but the popularity of the *Baker's Manual* and *Understanding Baking* was too much for the new book to make a difference. It only had one printing, and I wish I still had a copy to show you.

A few months later, in the spring of 1961, the Institute was ready to publish its own first book on professional cooking, needing once again to establish some consistencies in the lessons taught to the students in the bulging classrooms. If the baking instructors had different experiences and ideas about teaching baking, as we had thought, which the *Baker's Manual* and *Understanding Baking* helped to rectify, the cooking instructors were worse. It seemed to me that once the standardized recipes and procedures of Escoffier were put aside in light of teaching and learning more modern techniques and cooking recipes, inconsistencies and therefore chaos once again tried to rule the kitchens.

Mrs. Roth was determined to settle the chefs' arguments politely but firmly. She knew the Institute could not continue on its current path without constantly increasing the integrity of its curriculum. The larger the Institute became, and the more notable its graduates, the more demand there was to constantly improve the curriculum and the teaching tools used to deliver it.

Naturally, I was selected as one of the faculty to help on this new project, along with Leroi (the King) Folsom, who was teaching storeroom operations at that time. My writing background and eye for simple detail was a great asset for the new project. Along with Folsom's vast knowledge of cooking and serving the world's finest foods we would become the perfect duo, and soon the project was underway.

I'm not sure how—I am fairly certain Mrs. Roth had everything to do with it—but *Restaurants & Institutions,* already a leading hospitality business magazine of the time, had agreed to run a monthly column on the activities of the Institute. It was an easy sell for her to convince the editor, Jane Wallace, to begin running the articles on professional cooking that Leroi and I began to write.

The articles carried the name "Practical Cooking and Baking for Schools and Institutes," co-written by Leroi Folsom and Joseph Amendola of the Culinary Institute of America in New Haven, Connecticut. They ran every month for two years.

At the end of the two years Leroi, the CIA, and I published the series into a textbook, which became the first published textbook under the CIA's name. Today there are several CIA books, and several editions of what was to become *The Professional Chef,* the project Leroi and I started in 1961.

Rich Danish Dough

Method	(100 lb. Flour Basis) lb.	oz.	Ingredients	(Gallon Basis) lb.	oz.
Cream together:	22		Granulated sugar	4	
	14		Shortening	2	8
	1		Salt		3
	2	12	Nonfat dry milk		8
	22		Whole eggs	4	
			Flavor (to suit)		
Dissolve together and add:	46		Cold water	8	5
				(4 qts.)	
	8	4	Yeast	1	8
Add and mix in, being careful not to overmix:	78		Bread flour (variable)	14	
Temperature after mixing (78–80°F):	22		Cake flour (variable)	4	
Weight:	216			39	
Roll-in*:	54		Shortening	9	12
Total weight:	270			48	12
				(780 oz.)	

*Danish dough is a rolled-in or laminated dough with fat rolled sequentially through hundreds of layers of fat and dough. The roll-in process for Danish is similar to puff pastry, but with fewer turns and folds.

Sweet Yeast Dough

Method	(100 lb. Flour Basis)		Ingredients	(Gallon Basis)	
	lb.	oz.		lb.	oz.
Mix together	20		Sugar	4	
	20		Shortening	4	
	1	5	Salt*		4 1/4
	20		Whole eggs	4	
	2		Malt Syrup		6
	5		Nonfat dry milk	1	
Add to above:	80		Bread flour	16	
	20		Cake flour	4	
Dissolve together and add on top of flour. Mix dough in usual manner for sweet dough.	42	8	Water (variable)	8 (4 qts.)	5
Temperature after mixing: 80°F. Fermentation: about 1 3/4 hours.	8		Yeast	1	6
Total weight:	218	13		43 (695 1/4 oz.)	7 1/4

Peanut Butter Filling

Method	(Batch) lb.	oz.	Ingredients
Cream together:	2		Light brown sugar
	1	8	Peanut butter
		1/2	Salt
	1	2	Shortening
Add gradually while creaming:		8	Whole eggs
Add in gradually:	1	8	Water
Then add in and mix smooth:	3	8	Toasted cake crumbs
Total weight:	10	2 1/2	(162 1/2 oz.)

Orange Filling

Method	(Batch) lb.	oz.	Ingredients
Mix together thoroughly:	3		Macaroon coconut
	3		Granulated sugar
	2		Ground whole oranges
		12	Melted shortening or margarine
		12	Vol-Tex egg product
		12	Water (variable)
Total weight:	10	4	(164 oz.)

Guest chef Paul Laesecke visits Joe Amendola for ice carving at the Culinary Institute of America.

Ice Carving Made Easy

By the mid-1960s the reputation of the CIA had grown around the country as an institution that taught students all they needed for successful careers in the foodservice industry. Our cooking and baking curriculums had evolved over the previous twenty years to include multiple aspects of American, international, and classical cuisine and service to a point where students were exposed to hundreds if not thousands of individual recipes and baking formulas, as well as the skills required to reproduce them successfully. After two years at the institute, graduates could confidently demonstrate proficiencies in the skills and knowledge required for successful careers as cooks and bakers leading to positions as chefs and pastry chefs after a few more years of additional experience and training.

Since its inception in 1946 the Institute has been driven to constantly improve its curriculum and the courses it contains to continuously offer students the most comprehensive program possible given our limited two-year schedule (after all, it took me a dozen years or more to be exposed to the same amount of learning and practice a typical Institute student would receive in our classrooms and cooking/baking laboratories). That was the real reason why we started inviting guest chefs and pastry chefs to the Institute from time to time—to give the students a different way of looking at things or a new way practicing some part of the craft.

Notable chefs like Hans Bueschkens from Canada, Joseph Donan, who was a student of Escoffier, and Louis Szathmary from Chicago's The Bakery would walk our halls and lead our classes with lectures and demonstrations on modern cooking and baking skills. In later years international moguls like Roger Verger and Paul Bocuse not only taught in our classes, but became close friends and supporters of the Institute and the level of quality culinary education we always strove to achieve. Great chefs, seasoned instructors, and a full curriculum was the recipe for success for many Institute students and subsequent graduates.

There was one aspect of fine cuisine and hospitality, however, that the Institute didn't offer at one time because it was thought to be too much of a specialization to teach to all the students. Though ice carvings were already considered an integral part of elegant buffet displays, the practice of carving them was thought to be too intense to teach young culinarians. We were already challenged with teaching students what they needed to know in order to give them the basic skills and knowledge required for successful careers, let alone what we may have wanted to teach them.

I had always considered myself to be a student first and instructor second. Ever since my apprenticeship days with my uncle, I longed to learn new things and was grateful for the ability to achieve new skills. So I took up the challenge of learning to do ice carvings myself, and in that way I could then teach the skills to the more motivated students who shared my passion for knowledge and perfecting our craft.

Unfortunately, there were no books on ice carving at that time, but I decided to try it out by myself and bought my first set of carving chisels and saws from a local hardware store in New Haven. They weren't actually ice-carving tools as we have today, but the flat and v-shaped wood chisels I did buy served me well when I was just learning to do carvings.

I started out making bowls and soon improved to a point where I was able to weave form into their shapes as though they were made out of stretched rope or woven straw. Wine glasses were easy after a while, and soon I was practicing carving my first swan out of a 300-pound block of ice. It looked more like a pelican than a swan, but we all have to start somewhere.

Back then I could get a single block of ice from a local ice company for 50 cents. Today they're more than $50; that's inflation for you. And for 50 cents, I would have to go and pick up the ice myself. Delivery was extra.

There was a little space on the ground in the rear of the main building on Prospect Street where I began to carve my ice. After completion, I would leave it there for the next day and let the carving melt away slowly as dozens of students and faculty walked by on their way to and from classes.

Some of the students would stop and ask me if I would teach them how to do ice carvings. I said I would be happy to, but that it had to be after classes or on the weekend since there was no room in the curriculum for another lengthy class. To compensate, however, I told them I wouldn't charge them anything for the classes. After all, I was only learning how to carve ice myself, and would welcome the company as I chipped away at those huge blocks, turning them, I hoped, into glimmering, elegant forms.

But you know what? I had few actual takers, although many enquiries. Especially when I explained it would have to be after class or on the weekends, they all looked at me like I was crazy. Perhaps I was.

Then one day George Weising, a professional ice carver from Bridgeport, visited the school. He had built a solid business out of carving ice for the rich families in southern Connecticut including Bridgeport and New Haven, and was looking to expand his business.

When I told him I was having trouble getting students to take lessons he quipped it was probably because of my own inadequacies as an ice carver. I took it as the insult it was intended to be with great humility, and also with an open mind to hear what he had to say next.

He offered to teach a class of students himself if they would drive to Bridgeport and then pay $50 for a three-week class. He would arrange to meet the students at his shop in Bridgeport on Sunday mornings and show them one different ice-sculpturing technique each week.

It was he that I thought was crazy. At the Institute I couldn't get students to learn for free, after classes or on a Saturday, and he expected them to drive all the way to Bridgeport, pay for the classes out of their own pockets, and to do so on Sundays. I would have taken bets that he would have absolutely no luck at all.

To my surprise the first class of ten students was put together in only a few days after posting the notice. We even made them pay in advance to make sure they were serious about taking the class, knowing they would be on their own for transportation. They seemed eager to do so, and thought it was a bargain. (How could it be a bargain when I was doing it for free right in their own backyard?)

What I learned for the first time, and have witnessed many times since then, is that value perceived is value charged. In other words when you offer a service or product for free, customers cannot perceive real value for them, and lose interest right away. If you charged a moderate fee then their anticipation would be moderately higher; if, however, you charged an enormous fee, in comparison to the others, and imposed complications on attendance, then the perceived value for participation would increase in direct proportion to the value charged. Amazing, isn't it?

Needless to say a few weeks later we all (me included) drove to Bridgeport to meet Mr. Weising at his shop, and were prepared to learn about carving ice for fifty bucks each (also including me).

I remember the first thing he carved was a bowl, as I had already done days earlier; then he moved to carve a vase from another block of ice placed on top of an icy pedestal, which he managed with little effort (and much less verbal instruction). Then he turned to me and said I should demonstrate to them how to carve a swan out of the third piece of ice he had arranged for that day's lessons.

I was surprised, but I didn't hesitate to pick up the chisels he was using and go about demonstrating the proper techniques to accomplish the task.

He, the students, and I were equally impressed with the outcome. The figure actually looked like a swan, not a pelican as my earlier examples, floating gracefully on a pool of water as though it were plucked right off of a story book's cover. The ease by which I was able to perform such

Student at Culinary Institute of America working with Joe Amendola on ice carving.

a miracle with ice told me that others could learn to do so just as quickly and effortlessly if given proper instructions and guidance in doing so.

So I wrote the manuscript for what has become *Ice Carving Made Easy* and had one of my students take the pictures. Unfortunately, as before, I had no publisher who was even a bit interested in publishing a book on ice carving; many of them didn't even know what ice carvings were or how they were made. I suppose they thought it was magic and not skill that turns huge ice cubes into flowing figurines.

Finally I met a Mrs. Dahl, who had her own small publishing company and agreed to print my book if I paid for all the costs. It wasn't what I wanted, but I knew it was the best offer I was going to get.

So we did it. Dahl Publishing printed five hundred copies of *Ice Carving Made Easy* in the winter of 1962, and charged me $1,000 for doing so.

That was a lot of money back then, but I was sure I could sell them all if only for $5 a piece. I thought it might take me a while, but I was willing to make the investment.

They were all sold out in less than a month or so after I received them.

It happened right afterwards that I was visiting in Chicago during the National Restaurant Association (NRA) convention that year and met Richard Brown, who was in charge of educational services for the NRA at that time. I mentioned to him my experiment with the book, and the success of the initial printing, and asked if he and the NRA would be interested in publishing it themselves.

I think more out of a sense of service to the Institute, which I mentioned had already amassed quite a reputation, and possibly because the NRA's educational institute was still so young back then, he took me up on the idea. Within six months the second edition of *Ice Carving Made Easy* was published by the NRA in hardback copy and has enjoyed several printings ever since.

I'd like to think it was because of what we did at the Institute and my book that has since added Ice carving to culinary school curriculums around the world. I'm still called on to judge ice carving competitions wherever I go, and am gratified to see how far advanced the art form is today.

But Dr. Frankenstein—I don't need a buddy! This depicts a slightly calmer version of the "Horror" position. It shows fear with a bit less emotion. (From Joe Amendola's book *More Than Words Can Express,* unpublished)

More Than Words Can Express

My last book never got published, but appears in parts throughout this book. Hand gestures was my way of having fun through writing, and I have to say I enjoyed every minute of writing it.

In all of my travels, including my international travels, hand gestures were always prevalent in the many different cultures I experienced and the people I got to meet and make friends with. Many of the gestures I saw are universal, so I decided to write them all down in a book, which I titled *More Than Words Can Express*.

At that time, Douglas Forshey was a friend and neighbor of the Institute who had always had an affinity toward drawing. What I could do was write down all the gestures I wanted captured in the book's pages, and Douglas could draw them out as illustrations for the booklet. Some of my attempts at drawing, I must admit, looked nothing like the ones that ended up in the book, but I guess they were close enough to give Douglas the directions he needed. It's nice to know where your talents lay and where they end, and drawing is not one of my strengths.

When we were finished I tried to get it published many times, but no publisher was interested enough in doing so. Since it wasn't anything that we could use at the CIA, even the Institute's publishers turned me down. It didn't upset me though; I had done it more for fun anyway, and I'll never regret doing so. It's ironic in a way that some of them appear in this book, but then again it is the story of my life; and humor, I hope, will always have a place in my heart. I hope you enjoy what you see.

Thus it is evident that not everything you do that is innovative gets you recognition; you just have to keep on trying until you find the right niche for the right product for the right market. Maybe one day *More Than Words Can Express* will appear in its entirety, and maybe it won't.

But I don't give up. This book may or may not be my last. You never know; the journey is still continuing. The following text is pulled from the *More Than Words Can Express* manuscript.

Introduction

Let me first assure the reader that this discussion on hand gestures is not to be taken too seriously. It has no hidden message and is not intended to belittle any particular ethnic group. Rather, it is a compilation of colorful hand gestures used throughout the world by all expressive people. It might be referred to simply as a very humorous "hand dictionary," not as a dictionary to hold in one's hand, but a dictionary, literally, of "hands."

America is a melting pot—many people, many cultures, varied customs—and many of us, perhaps without any real conscious thought, have used our hands in expressive gestures at one time or another. I hope to awaken in the reader a sense of the humor and variety of hand gestures, and their importance as a link that exists between all people.

"The hands—wherein lies a tale" are indeed two of the most expressive parts of the human body. They can express anger, sorrow, joy, dismay, and indifference, among other emotions. Confucius said, "A picture is worth a thousand words"—possibly a hand gesture is worth that and many more!

Hand gestures are universally understood and are by no means a new innovation. Centuries ago, in the Coliseum in Rome, where a savage sport was the fight to the death between the gladiators, a man's fate was in the hands of the spectators, or to be more specific, in their thumbs— thumbs up meant he lived, thumbs down, he dies!

In more recent years, the now world-famous "V" for Victory sign sported by Winston Churchill became as much a part of his persona as seeing him with his cigar. Many examples of the significance of hand gestures throughout the ages are available. It is interesting to speculate on the meaning behind them and to rate how they survive the years as compared with written and spoken languages, which must be changed and updated periodically.

The hands envelop a language understood by all people. One does not necessarily need to speak the language to be able to understand the police officer directing traffic, for instance. His or her hand signals can become a veritable symphony of signs, fascinating to behold.

The world of religion many times relies on the hands for meaning— the folding of hands in prayer and reverence, the using of hands in blessing. Pontius Pilate washed his hands to indicate his absolvement of blame. Hand gestures and religion will be discussed in a later section.

I have incorporated a few pages of facts relevant to the "silent language" to assist the reader in understanding some of the origins. However, the main text has been written and illustrated for your enjoyment—so, on with the show.

A Brief History of Sign Language

The history of sign language is as old as mankind itself. Sign language is making gestures that are understood by visual means rather than by verbal means. The ability to express our thoughts and feelings by a mere gesture can be traced back to the earliest stages of man. A baby makes his needs known, his likes and dislikes, by kicking, waving his arms, eating his fist, and so on before he is able to utter one verbal word.

Which, in reality, came first, the spoken word or use of silent language? This has presented an interesting problem for anthropologists for many years. It has been theorized that the needs of different peoples of the world to communicate with one another gave birth to most of our sign language as we know it today. If we define language as the ability of people to communicate with other people, I think we must assume that both the spoken language and sign language developed simultaneously, but independently, as they are based on the function of different muscles. The spoken word gradually developed, as did the gestures. When strangers met strangers, they may not have always encountered doubt as to what the gestures meant. Many gestures were instinctive, and just as instinctively understood.

At the beginning of recorded history it was already common to pantomime or mimic—meaning a "dumb show,"—and dancing accompanied this mimicry. Long ago Indians told tales of romance, war, and disaster through the play of their bodies and hands. More than 2,000 years ago Sicily was constantly colonized by Greeks, Romans, Vandals, and Goths, all of whom did not speak the same dialect, thus sign language must have been used. Most of southern Italy, especially Naples, is an area where the silent language of gestures still flourishes. Travel books written at the turn of the century record people sitting in the stalls in theaters carrying on lively conversations with those sitting in the boxes, using nothing else but their eyes and hands.

With the opening up of the New World by white settlers came a need to communicate with the native Indian tribes, and for tribe to communicate with tribe. This resulted in the beginning of what we know as the Indian sign language.

Sign Language in Religion

Perhaps the most significant form of communicating messages with the hands is to be found in religious ceremonies, kept alive by tradition through the ages and depicted in painting, frescoes, sculptures, and reliefs—the outstretched hands, palms up in offering, hands closed in prayer, outstretched hands, palms down in blessing. The eloquence in the "hands" of religion speak far more clearly than words.

There are gestures originating in religious rites that have reappeared in customs and ceremonies—to raise the right hand when taking an oath, ending with the spoken phrase, "So help me God," or the hand raised, meaning "Peace." The outstretched hands of the priest holding an offering became the silent plea of the beggar, or a plea for mercy.

The use of the hands in religion is explicit, encompassing eternal symbols unchanged in their simplicity and meaning.

Folklore and Sign Language

There is a story taken from the oldest stories in Sanskrit, "Ocean Streams of Stories," the Tale of the Prince and the Ivory Carver's Daughter.

It tells the tale of a handsome prince and his friend who go hunting. After a long chase through the forest, they stop at a lake, where they see a beautiful maiden with her attendants. The prince and the maiden look at each other and instantly fall in love. He wonders who she might be, and she, guessing his thoughts, takes a lotus from her garland of flowers and puts it in her ear. She twists the lotus to form a "tooth leaf," then she takes another lotus and puts it on her head; finally, she places her hand over her heart. She and her attendants depart, and the prince and his friend go home. The prince is sad because he has not understood the girl's message, but his friend is able to tell him the meaning of the signs. The lotus in her ear tells where she lives. By lifting the lotus, she reveals her name: "Lotus Jewel." By twisting the lotus into a "tooth leaf" ornament she tells him her father is an ivory carver. By placing her hand over her heart, she tells him it is his.

The prince and his friend travel to the town where Lotus Jewel lives and persuade the maiden's old nurse to take a message to her. When the old woman returns, she has ten distinct finger marks on her cheeks. She tells the prince that her mistress "struck her with two hands smeared with camphor." It is a coded message, the prince's friend explains: ten white finger marks mean ten moonlit nights that are unfavorable to secret meetings; therefore, they must wait.

After ten days have passed, the old woman returns to the prince, this time with three red finger marks across her breast. This means that the maiden cannot see the prince for another three days.

A number of sign language messages are exchanged before the lovers are able to live happily ever after.

Some messages in silent language are liable to lead to misunderstandings, resulting in some very interesting stories. The following is one of many.

A monk comes before his king with the monetary tribute from his village, but he has an idea how to avoid payment. He challenges the king and his ministers to answer two questions that he will put to them in sign language. If they fail to give him the correct answers, they will forfeit the tribute. The challenge is accepted, but the sign language baffles the king and his ministers.

There is a traveling peasant in the crowd and he asks permission to try. The monk begins again—he opens his hand and holds the palm before the peasant's face. The peasant replies by showing the monk his fist. Next the monk lets his five fingers droop. The peasant opens his fist and holds his fingers upward. The monk has to admit that the peasant has given him the right answer and pays him.

Later the king asks the peasant how he did it, and the peasant explains, "When the monk opened his hand and held it to my face, he meant, 'I slap your face,' I showed him my fist, which meant, 'I punch your nose.' When the monk let his fingers droop, he was saying, 'I'll seize your throat.' When I put my fingers up, I was saying, 'I'll seize you from below.'" Then the king asks the monk for his explanation.

The monk says, "When I held my open hand against his face, I said, 'you worship five times a day—right?' He answered 'yes' by clenching his fist. When I let my fingers droop, I was asking, 'Why does the rain come down from heaven?' He replied by putting his hand, fingers up, saying, 'So that the grass may grow from the earth.' "

It was a misunderstanding, but what interesting explanations for those hand gestures.

Traditions and Customs around the World

Generally speaking, it is assumed that the Latin nations are more expressive in their gesticulations, owing to their temperament, than say, the Scandinavians or British. True, many Englishmen may conform to their traditional image, but interestingly, the majority of these people will make just as many gestures to make their point as their more flamboyant Latin neighbors. Spend a few minutes at "Speakers Corner" in Hyde Park, London and watch the orators in action—stabbing the air, pounding their fists, in other words, making themselves understood with their hands.

The following are examples of how gestures have influenced language, in that they explain the meaning and origin of some common used phrase

- To "buttonhole" someone is defined in the Oxford dictionary as "to detain a reluctant listener by holding on to his button." This stems from the habit orators had of holding fast to a button of one of their audience members.

- In Elizabethan England it was the custom to bite one's thumb at an enemy to show anger or displeasure.
- The Orientals have an idiom, as do Americans, "to save face," originating from covering the face from shame; the hands cover the face as a mask would.

Gestures have enriched the languages of all nations, but not every nation has the same meaning for an identical gesture. For example, a gesture indicating the cracking of a louse between the thumbnails, in Spain simply means "you are a louse," whereas in parts of Germany, the same gesture means "stop nagging me."

Many times we see someone tap their head, usually silently referring to a second party. To an Englishman such a gesture means "what a terrific brain." To a Jew, when accompanied by the word "toches," it means the person has made himself look foolish, and when an American does it, he usually means the person referred to is a little mad.

Snapping the fingers is a universal gesture with various meanings. An Englishman will use it to mean that "it is not worth it," or to mean that something was accomplished quite suddenly. In Central Europe snapping fingers are used to summon a waiter, whereas in Anglo Saxon countries it is frowned upon as a means of summoning a waiter; simply raising a finger is preferred. To summon a waiter in Africa, you rap on the table, and in the Middle East you clap your hands. Snapping the fingers in Naples can mean a number of things, depending on the situation—joy, refusal, even just feeling carefree. Even in today's world, snapping the fingers is a means of keeping time to the beat of music.

In many countries there is no discrimination between using the right or left hand, although the right hand is used for a handshake. Among Moslems in parts of India, the left hand is considered "unclean." Only the right hand is used to offer or accept gifts and coins.

Smiling is not in the accepted sense a "gesture," but still it plays its part in silent language. It can be a ritual as opposed to an instinctive indication of happy mood. In Japan, for instance, smiling is a social duty for many, even when referring to sad events.

An individual looking for a fight in parts of Germany or Austria will put his hat back to front or will pull the peak of his cap over his eyes (just as knights of old pulled down their visors before going into battle). Most Englishmen or Americans would remove their jackets preparatory to a fight. In early American times, a boy would put a chip of wood on his shoulder, daring his opponent to knock it off—hence the expression, "he has a chip on his shoulder."

Perhaps one of the most elegant gestures of preliminary fighting was the slap in the face challenging an opponent to a duel, or the duelist might simply say, "Sir, consider yourself slapped in the face," and the insult would then need to be avenged with blood.

Each era in time had its own form of greeting. Today we raise an arm in friendly greeting, a symbolic gesture. When people carried weapons, they would raise a hand to show they were not hostile.

Today, in this era, the young have little patience with pantomime. Rather, they will shout their silent messages by means of buttons, messages on tee shirts, or the like. Perhaps this method is just as effective, but it is not nearly as interesting!

Pineapple Cheese Filling

| | (Batch) | | |
Method	lb.	oz.	Ingredients
Mix until smooth:	8		Baker's cheese
	2		Sugar
		8	Melted margarine or shortening
		1	Salt
		12	Whole eggs
	2		Pineapple, drained, crushed
Total weight:	13	5	(213 oz.)

Pineapple Filling

Method	(Batch) lb.	oz.	Ingredients
Bring to a boil:	5		Crushed pineapple
	1		Granulated sugar
Dissolve together, then add to the boiling mix, stirring constantly		3	Cornstarch
until thick and clear:	1		Water
Add and mix smooth:	1		Cake crumbs (variable)
Total weight:	8	3	(131 oz.)

Cinnamon Cream Filling

Method	(Batch) lb.	oz.		Ingredients
Cream to medium lightness:	5			Powered sugar
	2	8		Fleischmann's Red Band shortening
		8		Cake flour
		8		Cinnamon (variable)
		2		Cocoa
Then add slowly and mix smooth:	1	8		Egg whites
Total weight:	10	2	(162 oz.)	

Reader's Notes and Thoughts

Marge Amendola in 1945.

Marge Amendola: Stories from around the World

Naturally, another great benefit of all of my travels around the United States and the world was the opportunity for my beautiful wife Marge to come with me, as long as she wasn't needed at home to raise our two children, Joseph and Jeanette. We tried particularly hard for her to join me whenever I had to go on one of my international trips. And we had a great time being together wherever we went.

So while I was busy making or building culinary relationships, either for the American Culinary Federation (ACF), the CIA, or with some prestigious culinary school in Europe or Asia, Marge would keep a little journal so that we could both remember the fun we had during those trips as much as the business contacts and deals we made.

It's strange, but today I remember more clearly the things Marge wrote in those pages than the many hours of business discussions and deals. We had a ball, and I want to share our experiences abroad with you. We visited many places, but here are stories surrounding our Korea, China, and Egypt visits to give you just a taste of what we experienced, and will remember for the rest of our lives. As you read, be aware that Marge is your narrator throughout this chapter, and I am referred to as "Joe."

Republic of Korea (1985)

Korea—"The Land of the Morning Calm" is perhaps one of the best-kept travel secrets in today's shrinking world. Seoul, the capital of South Korea, is the hub of this fascinating country, a veritable jigsaw puzzle of modern skyscrapers and old palaces, beautiful gardens, markets, and shops and more shops.

We were met at the airport on our arrival in Seoul by Mr. Seoung Soon Lee, food and beverage manager of the Hotel Lotte. This young man had certainly found his true vocation. He was warm and friendly and very, very good at his job!

The Hotel Lotte complex was somewhat overwhelming when we first arrived. We really did not expect to see this kind of luxury and sophistication in Seoul—a blend of the comforts of today's world with all the true elegance of yesterday's traditions.

Dining at the Hotel Lotte was a marvelous experience. It had thirty-one restaurants and bars, each with its own unique charm and atmosphere, and from personal experience, I can attest to the excellence of the food. We were really honored to be invited to sit at the chef's table one day for lunch, where we enjoyed many of the traditional Korean dishes. We were pretty proficient with chopsticks; however, at this luncheon we were equipped with silver chopsticks, and if you have ever tried to pick up pieces of octopus with these slippery silver chopsticks—well, I would suggest a practice session first, a long one!

The Po Suk Jung Korean restaurant in the Hotel Lotte was a must—not only for the excellent Korean food, but also for the entertainment. The exquisite traditional costumes and the beauty and grace of the performers made the history of Korea come alive in music and dance.

Until 1392, Seoul was a small town that for centuries had existed in a picturesque basin formed by the low hills in central Korea. It was in the year 1392 that Teajo, the first king of the Yi Dynasty, selected Seoul as the new capital. He was responsible for turning the town into a walled city, and built many palaces, temples, gardens, and fortresses, many of which remain today for us all to enjoy. One of the main attractions from that era is the Great South Gate (Tong-dae-mun), which is now located in the middle of downtown and which, incidentally, makes a great landmark for lost tourists.

The population of Seoul today exceeds nine million, and it is still growing. One thing we couldn't help but notice was how very industrious the South Korean people were. The two key words we would use to describe these people are friendly and industrious.

The National Folklore museum was certainly worth the visit, as was the Ch'ang-dok-kung Palace and Secret Garden. We also visited the Seoul Tower, which rises high above the city. Looking down from this great height on the city and its surroundings is akin to looking down on any American or European busy city, full of lights, life, and hustle and bustle. It gave us a strange feeling to look to the north and see a black void—North Korea; we felt almost as though a visible line had been drawn dividing the light from the dark. Incidentally, the final ascent to the Tower is exceptionally steep, if you are getting on in years, getting to the top is quite a *fait accompli,* but we made it, with just a very few gasps to spare!

One morning we arose at 4 AM—after retiring at approximately 1 AM—which just goes to prove that when exciting things are happening, who needs sleep! Anyway, at 4 AM we met Mr. Lee and we went off to the vegetable and fruit market, and what a market it was! It was comparatively new, and enormous. Miles and miles of watermelons, fruit, and vegetables. But perhaps most interesting were the people, buying and haggling, and always, busy, busy, and always with a smile.

Next, we went on to the fish market—Joe's favorite. Actually I almost felt that we were the main attraction—what were these two crazy occidentals doing at such an hour in this smelly, fishy, fantastic place, taking pictures with the enormous crabs, all of six-feet wide, and huge octopi (I don't think it is "octopuses") that make you believe that Captain Nemo and his creatures of the deep really did exit. It was an experience we shall never forget, and neither will our sneakers!

Later that day we went to the outdoor silk market, rows and rows of stalls with the most beautiful silks imaginable. It looked like a scene from the Arabian Nights—the colors were more beautiful than a rainbow. Then we went to the outdoor food market, a veritable feast of smells and sights. Exotic-looking foods were everywhere; it would have been wonderful to stop and taste everything, but

I am sure it would have taken us at least two days. Again one could not help noticing the warmth and friendliness of the people. It is often said that when you give a smile it is returned tenfold, and in this country it was really so.

Mr. Lee took us to his home to meet his lovely family and his "Yobo"—interpreted into English this means *wife, sweetheart,* or anyone dear to you. Joe loves to come up with his interpretation of things; spelled backwards it's "o'boy"! We all went out to dinner and had Peking duck; prepared tableside, it is served on a wafer-thin pancake with the appropriate garnish and sauce, then rolled up and eaten with the fingers. What a marvelous taste treat that was.

A familiar restaurant sight in capitals around Asia is the sign reading "Korean Barbecue." In Korean its true name is *Pulgogi;* it consists of strips of beef, ordered by choosing from various grades, roasted on a grill ingeniously inset on the tabletop. The meat is first marinated in a mixture of soy sauce, sesame, and spices, and gives off an enticing aroma as it cooks. A variety of sliced vegetables accompanies the beef, and this is usually served with a clear seaweed soup and white rice. Koreans like to roll the cooked beef with a dash of sesame paste into a leaf of lettuce and eat it much as the Japanese eat sushi.

No Korean meal is complete without *Kimchi.* This mixture of peppery, hot fermented cabbage, radishes, and vegetables is considered to be Korea's most unique dish. It is traditionally prepared in the winter months, when it is pickled in brine and stored underground in earthenware pots. Other interesting dishes to try are *Kalbi,* marinated short ribs, and *sinsollo,* a casserole of vegetables, eggs, and strips of meat and fish mixed with pine and ginkgo nuts. A century ago this dish was prepared only for royalty.

We particularly liked the Korean ginseng tea. The ginseng root is considered to be very healthful, and children are raised on this and flat, paper-thin strips of seaweed. For most of South Korea following the war, the rapid pace of development has given few people time to look back and consider their roots.

For most, the past is best forgotten as a time of poverty and suffering. Seoul was the site of the 1986 Asian Olympics, and before the time of our visit already they had constructed a beautiful coliseum and arena for this purpose. The country appeared to be in a great hurry to charge ahead into a better future, but still preserved in the traditions and culture of their forebears.

We left "The Land of the Morning Calm" with many wonderful memories of a beautiful country and genuinely loving and caring people.

Seu-Tang
(4 servings)

Ingredients

15	Medium shrimp
2	Scallions
1/2	Bunch watercress
7 c.	Water
2 tbs.	Soy sauce
1 tsp.	Salt
1/4 tsp.	Pepper

Method

1. Clean and wash shrimp, drain.
2. Cut scallions.
3. Clean and wash watercress, cut into 2 in. lengths.
4. Pour water into deep sauce pan, add soy sauce and salt, bring to boil over high heat.
5. Add shrimp, watercress, and scallion.
6. Sprinkle with pepper. Cook 10 min.

DO-MI-CHO-RIM
(Stewed Fish with Soy Sauce and Sugar)
(2 servings)

Ingredients

2 lb.	Snapper
2 tbs.	Sliced ginger
4	Cloves garlic
6 tbs.	Soy sauce
3 tbs.	Sugar
3 tbs.	Wine

Method

1. Clean snapper, cut crosswise into 5 pieces.
2. Slice garlic thinly.
3. Pour soy sauce in deep pan. Add sugar, wine, garlic, and ginger and bring to boil over medium heat.
4. Add snapper pieces, cook until liquid is thickened.
5. While cooking, baste several times.
6. Set in casserole and serve.

YAK-GWA
(Fried Cookie)

Ingredients

2 c.	Flour
1/4 tsp.	Salt
3 tbs.	Sesame oil
1 tbs.	Ginger juice
3 tbs.	Honey
2 tbs.	Wine
1 c.	Water
3 c.	Oil
1/2 c.	Honey
1/2 c.	Sugar
1 tbs.	Ground pine nuts
1 tbs.	Cinnamon

Method

1. Place flour in bowl; add salt and sesame oil and rub with hands.
2. Mix well; add ginger juice, honey, wine, and water and mix well into dough. Squeeze several times.
3. Remove dough onto flour-coated board; flatten.
4. Roll dough out 1/3 inch thick; cut with cutter into rounds.
5. Fry pieces of dough in deep oil in pan over low heat slowly until brown.
6. Pour water in pan. Add honey and sugar. Bring to boil.
7. Mix well over low heat, add fried Yak-gwa and coat with mixture.
8. Sprinkle with pine nuts and cinnamon, serve.

Hong Kong (1983)

The excitement began when we flew into Hong Kong (Fragrant Harbor), commonly known as the "Pearl of the Orient"—this is certainly an apt description. Flying in at night, the view brought to mind a magnificent collection of glittering jewels set on a dark blue velvet backdrop. Flying in during the daylight hours, we would have been greeted by the beauty of the surrounding hills and land-shapes, and then the almost physical shock of flying low over the myriad hotels and buildings.

Hong Kong is an excellent natural harbor; its size and strategic location have made it a gateway between West and East, which is probably why we noted such a cosmopolitan flavor, both in its people and its cuisine.

When we arrived in Hong Kong we were escorted to the Excelsior Hotel, which was conveniently located next door to the Hong Kong World Trade Centre Club. Upstairs in our room, which boasted a magnificent view of the harbor, we were brought refreshing Chinese tea. I guarantee that even though you may be a "dyed in the wool" coffee drinker, this tea could change your drinking habits. The drinking of tea is said to date back over 2,000 years in Chinese history. Tea was introduced from China to Japan in the seventh century and to Britain in the eighteenth century. Tea drinking is considered an art, and for the people of Hong Kong a form of relaxation. In fact, during our visit, a museum in Hong Kong, "Flagstaff House," was being renovated prior to becoming a tea museum.

That evening we had dinner at the World Trade Centre Club, a private club under the direction of Miss Annie Wu. We will digress here a while to fill you in just a little regarding Miss Wu. Miss Wu was a dynamic personality with some of the most progressive and original ideas we had heard in many a year. She was ably assisted by her staff, Killy Lee, William Wu, and David Ng., to name just three among many, because Annie's enthusiasm was contagious. We found ourselves wanting to know more and do more when she spoke so knowledgeably on tourism and culinary training. The dinner that evening, better yet we should call it a banquet, was beautifully presented, the ambience was restful and gracious. During dinner a young woman played for us on a "butterfly piano," an

Joe meets with Chinese cooks during one of his trips.

exquisite instrument that we were allowed to try our hand at. The dinner ran to nine courses along with the inevitable tea.

The wine served with the dinner was Dynasty wine, a very light, rather dry white wine with a lovely delicate flavor that complemented the Chinese cuisine beautifully. Our first course was Dim-Sum, spring rolls, shrimp dumplings, pork dumplings, and onion cake. The second course was deep-fried boneless spareribs with pepper sauce.

Next came a delicious winter melon soup. Then steamed grouper with bean sauce. Next were string beans with chopped beef and garlic with hot sauce. Then Tan Tan noodles with beef sinew; the Chinese always finish their main courses with some form of noodles or rice. Dessert was mango pudding, and petit fours made with coconut, egg yolks, and dates. Finally—so that we didn't leave hungry—we were served ice cream bon bons dipped in mint-flavored chocolate, served on toothpicks in a miniature brass Chinese cooking kettle so they resembled charcoal nuggets.

Well, this was our initiation into what was to prove to be an exciting culinary excursion in Hong Kong.

Dare we say there are other interesting things to do in Hong Kong besides eating? For instance, we took the ferry across to Kowloon for 70 cents—that's First Class—to shop and visit some of the other beautiful hotels. That is not to say that we did not shop on the Hong Kong side or that there are not just as many beautiful hotels, but the ferry ride was a pleasant experience. We zipped across amidst all the busy harbor traffic; it took about 7 minutes to cross, so we photographed some of the most spectacular views along the way.

Back to the cuisine—were we ever away from it? Hong Kong is a gastronomic delight, there is a restaurant in Hong Kong to satisfy everyone.

The following day we had lunch at Maxims Palace; this establishment was run by Annie Wu's father, Williams Wu. He also ran the Jade Gardens restaurant among his many endeavors, one of which was very popular in Tokyo, Japan. Maxims Palace was a wonder to behold. It sat 1,200 and resembled a huge elegant oriental banquet hall, complete with dragons, Chinese motifs, and magnificent chandeliers. It was a family-style restaurant and on a Sunday would do seven turnovers. It specialized in Dim Sun; most of us who enjoy Chinese food are familiar with Dim Sum and have been to Dim Sum restaurants in the United States. However, we were not quite prepared for this one. We sampled over forty varieties, and finally had to stop, but we were told that they serve as many as sixty varieties with unlimited combinations. We were fascinated by those shaped like fish and various animals. This is not merely good food, it is an art form.

No self-respecting visitor would go to Hong Kong without visiting Victoria Peak. It rises dramatically 1,809 feet above Hong Kong and provides a spectacular view of Hong Kong Harbor. You can reach it by tram (a funicular railway) or take a cab. This time we went up at night on the tram, and had dinner at the Tower Restaurant, with the most breathtaking view laid out before us. Coming down we took a cab, which is also quite an experience. If you have ever driven the Amalfi Drive in Italy, this is a similar experience, where everyone tends to breathe a secret sigh of relief on arrival. The Chinese foods of Hong Kong are comprised of primarily seven types: Cantonese, Shanghainese, Pekinese (Northern), Szechwan (hot), Chiu Chow, Fukienese, and Mongolian.

There is also Hakke food, eaten by the farmers in the New Territories and by the boat people of Aberdeen. One of the many luncheons held for us at the club was a press conference; among the guests was Mrs. Levin, wife of the American consulate, a very able chef in her own right. Mrs. Levin was at that time in the process of writing a cookbook, which we were most interested in. On a former visit to Hong Kong, Joe had occasion to witness the methods used by the chef making noodles. He was fascinated by the process and we discussed this one day at luncheon. Lo and behold, that evening during dinner the chef came out along with a portable table to demonstrate this skill. I don't think I have seen anything so interesting; they had Joe try his hand at it—much picture taking at this point—he really did a pretty good job, and had great fun.

Annie Wu accompanied us to a new venture called Discovery Bay. The best way to go was by hydrofoil. There we witnessed a unique, innovative lifestyle—not fully completed as of our visit, but still well on its way. It had a lovely beach—the sand was imported from Italy—and some of the most beautiful scenery in the area. It was really a world unto itself. Eventually it would have—besides homes, which were already built along with a restaurant, a club, and marina—one or two hotels and a gourmet restaurant. Discovery Bay appeared to us to be a community of the future, encompassing a free and natural living environment. The day we visited Discovery Bay we both remarked on its originality and the feeling of peace it gave. I think perhaps the words they themselves use to describe this project sum it up:

Sitting on these Flowered Hills,
I drink my Wine and Watch
The Birds fly into endless Space,
Their freedom is in the Sky,
Mine; the Earth and Home.
You have only to Come Along,
Come and See me Here.

Actually those words might easily be applied to all of Hong Kong, a place that you want to return to again and again for its beauty and excitement.

The next morning we were on our way to the People's Republic of China, via China Airlines, a remarkably comfortable airline with extremely polite stewards and stewardesses who were continually plying one with extras: fans, candy, handkerchiefs, drinks, and snacks, and whose outfits were very attractive. They were blue and white, and the stewardesses, when they were serving, wore very pretty white, ruffled, flower-embroidered aprons. Well, so much for high fashion in the skies!!

Arriving in Beijing (Peking) was exciting; we had a feeling of being somewhere totally different—a completely different world, a completely different culture, an exciting difference. As we drove from the airport to the hotel, there was no mistaking that complete difference. We were like children, fascinated by the sights and sounds of a new environment. The farmers in the fields—men and women—in their flat straw hats, workers in the rice paddies, the unbelievable fertility of the land they were working—we could hardly take it all in.

We saw bicycles, bicycles, and more bicycles, some balancing as many as eight chairs on the rear, pony- and horse-drawn carts with sleeping drivers, presumably the animals knew just where to go, the carts filled to overflowing, and baby carriages made from slats of wood, like wooden playpens on wheels. We heard the toot-tooting of horns because the motorized vehicles were outnumbered by the other forms of transportation. We beheld so many fascinating sights and sounds, too numerous to mention, and found that aura of the ancient culture wherever we looked. We felt like modern-day Marco Polos. A piece I had read somewhere kept running through my mind:

> In the Ancient East there is a Dragon,
> A dragon by the name of China.
> In the Ancient East there is a Race,
> They are the Dragons Descendants

Even the Great Wall resembles a huge dragon, but we will come to that part later on.

We arrived at the Jianguo Hotel in Beijing, and were met by Madame Ge, a lovely, happy woman who made us feel right at home. It is strange sometimes how language is no barrier with certain people (although in China an interpreter does help).

We had a delightful banquet with Madame Ge and her staff. The food, although Chinese, was subtly different from that in Hong Kong. Some of the ingredients were unfamiliar to us, but it was all delicious, and it was fascinating to watch the adept way in which we were served from the hung lazy Susan in the middle of the table. Served with chopsticks and ladle, every portion was exact.

We had traveled to Beijing with Chef Wong and his wife. Chef Wong had just retired, and was working as an advisor for the Jade Garden restaurants. His son was the number-one chef at the Jianguo Hotel, and evidently his father had taught him well. They were delightful people, and we give Chef Wong credit for learning to say "Good Morning" in English, whereas we did not fare so well with our Chinese, although we did learn the toast. There is a liquor called *Motai* that is usually served at banquets, and really, if one is not prepared for it, it can be quite a shock, albeit a pleasant one. On the subject of toasts, we did notice that the general rule appears to be that the first toast is given by the host. Also served with the food are soft drinks and beer brought around on a tray, and always, of course, tea.

One of our first side trips was to the Forbidden City (the Imperial Palace). Our guide's name was Romeo. He was a hard-working young man who was employed at the nearby International Club on Embassy Row. The Forbidden City, many, many years ago, was the permanent residence of the emperors of the Ming and Qing dynasties. Built in 1406–1420, it was the home of the emperors until 1911 when Pu-Yi, the last of the Qing emperors, was overthrown. A total of twenty-four emperors had lived there. The palace is awe-inspiring. As Joe said when he saw it, "The Taj Mahal has nothing on this."

There are numerous buildings on the grounds. The temples still have the thrones where the emperors gave audience, and lots of smaller houses surround these temples, which, according to Romeo, were for the wives. Joe felt they looked like the forerunners of present-day condominiums. The magnificence is hard to take in all at one time. The intricacy of the carved roofs, with their various animals and fish, the graceful charm of the buildings, and the colors that are still vibrant—one can stand there and imagine those emperors in their colorful robes walking up their special steps to the temples. Its is the kind of place, that, on coming out, you breathe a sigh and still can't comprehend what you just saw. During our travels we were struck also by how pleasant and shy and gentle the people were.

One of the most exciting trips was when we were taken to the Diaoqutal State House in Beijing. This is where heads of states are entertained. Here we were treated to what I can only describe as a royal banquet. The dishes were primarily soups and they had especially arranged the menu to include a dish from each of the Chinese provinces. It was a banquet we shall not easily forget; and, again, we all enjoyed each other's company—I believe because we were all sincere in our interests. If there are two main ingredients in bringing people close together, these we had in abundance—good food and hospitality.

Our next banquet was at the Peking Hotel, an older hotel with magnificently high ceilings. Again, the food and the company was of the very best. Fortunately, although there were many courses, each course was very small; otherwise, I think we would have been bouncing around like inflated balloons by this point.

The next excursion was to the place I had been waiting for, the Great Wall. We went with the Wongs and their son, with Johnny from the International Club, and with Roger, who had accompanied us to China to act as interpreter. By this time we were all great friends and had a lot of fun together. We went in a small van and had box lunches. There was also a mysterious bag that Johnny was carrying very carefully.

The trip to the Great Wall is an experience in itself. The Great Wall is like a huge undulating dragon, stretching further than the eye can see, twisting and turning, always following the contour of the land—the mountains and scenery are absolutely magnificent. Nowhere have I seen anything remotely resembling this terrain. As you climb into the mountains, every so often you catch a glimpse of the Wall, and each glimpse is more breathtaking than the last.

We climbed partway up the wall; it is much steeper than one imagines. In fact, coming down, if you are not careful, could become a nonstop flight. When we arrived at the spot where we felt we could go no further—Joe said he could have gone further if he had different shoes on—the mysterious bag was brought out. Chef Wong donned his chef's toque, his La Chaine de Rôtisseur medallion, and lo and behold here was a fully cooked Peking duck on a hook, a beautiful fish on a platter, and a bottle of Chinese wine. Roger, who took all the pictures, soon had Chef Wong and his son and Joe holding the duck, the fish, and the wine and posing for pictures. I doubt if this had ever been done on the Great Wall before. We caused quite a sensation.

Pretty soon we had an audience, with lots of people snapping pictures. I can imagine quite a few Chinese households now have our likenesses in their picture albums, and I overheard, from what sounded like an Australian, that we were probably doing commercials.

After this we moved to a quieter section of the Wall where Chef Wong proceeded to don an authentic mandarin outfit, from the hat down to the shoes. We shall always cherish these pictures taken on the Great Wall. For our box lunch we drove across to the other side of the Wall in Mongolia.

We were told that the astronauts claim that the Great Wall is the only edifice that they could see from outer space.

On the way back to the hotel, we stopped at Mings Tomb. Here the carvings of people and animals are larger than life, and what treasures this place does hold.

It would appear that we were forever eating, and actually we were. That night after dinner at the Peking Hotel, we went to the International Club on Embassy Row. This had been Westernized to accommodate the embassy people in the area. It was amazing to see what had been accomplished. Miss Annie Wu's hand in the matter was evident. Johnny was the maitre d' and was responsible for training the young girls, who learned very fast. We had baked Alaska that was scrumptious and Brazilian coffee. We watched the tableside service and flambéing, and it was every bit as well done as in many French restaurants.

Well, we were sad to leave Beijing, but anxious to visit Nanjing, which was at one time the capital of China.

We checked in at the new Jinling Hotel, where we were greeted warmly by Mr. Zhang, a most knowledgeable and intellectual man who was very proud of the beautiful hotel, and rightly so; the Jinling is thirty-seven stories high. We had a truly lovely suite, with all the comforts of home and then some. We were given tea and a box of confections that we were told were only made for "very special people." The hotel was modern, spacious, and equipped to international standards, but retained the hospitality and gentle courtesy of China's traditions.

Here we had yet another banquet in a beautiful room, and here we were introduced to more new dishes. We met Mr. Huang, the Director of Tourism, an exceptionally enthusiastic man. He was very proud of his beautiful city, and we could not agree more with him. Nanjing is a city of culture and scholarship. It is the capital of Jiangsu province, known as China's land of "Fish and Rice." Through Jiangsu province runs the Grand Canal, built 1,300 years ago to unite North and South China, and, along with the Great Wall, noted by Marco Polo as one of the major sights of China.

Mr. Huang told us a story about this Grand Canal. It seems that in those days the Emperor wanted to see a flower that only bloomed in May, and to do so he would have to travel from North to South. It was too great a distance to travel by horse and too tiring, so he had the canal built so that he could travel by Dragon Boat to see the flower.

Nanjing is a really beautiful city with tree-lined avenues and scenic lakes and parks. One of its main attractions is the Yangtse River's four-mile bridge. The bridge is a double-decker, double-track rail and road bridge started in 1960 and completed in 1968. It links the North and South of the Yangtse River. When we were there, the river was flooding in parts, which we understand it does every so often.

The people of Nanjing were very courteous and shy, and what struck us particularly was their total innocence, almost like children. They would stand for hours outside the gates of the hotel, just gazing at this strange edifice and watching the guests coming and going. As in Beijing, we were sorry to leave Nanjing. It was so beautiful, and there was so much still too see, but we promised our hosts—and ourselves—that we would come again.

We were off to Shanghai. Shanghai seems to conjure up romantic images of intrigue. Actually, it was the most Westernized of the three cities we visited, at least in some ways—clothing was more colorful and the people seemed a little more outgoing.

Early mornings we watched groups of people exercising or shadow boxing, very slow movements but very graceful; since neither of us is really into strenuous exercising, we felt this would be a good activity for us.

In Shanghai we stayed at the Jing Jang Hotel—don't you just love the musical names—a very old hotel with loads of charm. We had a very large suite with marvelous old furniture, big easy chairs, velvet draperies, and a huge bathtub. We also had a huge old bed; however, the mattress left much to be desired. It was fine for togetherness because you both rolled to the center automatically, conversely it was really hard to climb out. However, the hotel was a joy. Its old elevators—with someone running them—seemed so much faster than the self-controlled ones of today. They even had a "houseboy" on each floor.

Across the street at the Jing Jang Club we once again had a marvelous banquet, and interesting discussions with our host, Mr. Ren. Our companions were really concerned with seeing China grow and prosper. Here also we visited the State Guest House where visiting dignitaries are feted, and where Joe, as usual, visited the kitchens.

Miss Annie Wu also had an interest in the China Airlines Flight Kitchen in Shanghai. We toured the facility, which was surprisingly up-to-date, and sampled some of the desserts served on their flights. The airline's employees were so enthusiastic, and the young people so anxious and willing to learn.

The next morning, before our return to Hong Kong, we were treated to an authentic Chinese breakfast. Among other delicious dishes we were served "oily fingers," a type of long, fried dough, which were unbelievably good.

We were returning to Hong Kong, but China was still fresh in our hearts and minds. We hoped to someday return. This is a country with a culture and history beyond all imagining. Its scenery and beauty are astonishing. We can teach them so much, and in return they have so much to offer us; it was an experience we shall never forget.

In Hong Kong once again, we had been invited to stay at the Hilton, where we found a very warm welcome awaiting us from Mr. Michael Bamberg and his staff. Our accommodations were elegant to say the least. That evening we were invited to dine at the Eagles Nest. We often speak of the *piece d' resistance*—this had to be it. The table setting, the services, and the food preparation were exceptional, not to mention the superb view of the harbor. There were definitely artists at work here—artists skilled at vegetable carving and in combining dishes in originality. So much thought is given to the smallest detail. This, I thought, must be perfection.

Then came our last day. Our hosts tried to persuade us to stay one more day. I seconded the motion; unfortunately, it was not carried by Joe.

Wait, the excitement was not yet over. In the United States we've all heard of "Good Morning America," but have you heard of "Good Morning Hong Kong"? Joe appeared as a guest, and his every word was translated into Chinese. He showed slides of the Culinary Institute and, as usual, did his promotional job for the old school.

Meanwhile, back at the hotel, yours truly was frantically getting in that last minute shopping in this shopping mecca of the world. Then it was off in the Daimier, to the airport, and back to Hyde Park, New York. But, we hope to someday return; there is just so much more to do, more people to talk to, more great places to eat at—we didn't even scrape the surface.

Egypt (1985)

We had just spent four glorious days in Athens, feasting our minds and our eyes on Greek antiquities and the glories of legendary gods and goddesses while feasting our bodies on what the gods of Greek cuisine prepared for us. We were looking forward to our first glimpse of Cairo from the plane, but this was to be denied, since we landed in a rare sandstorm. It was a decidedly eerie introduction to the fabled land of the pharaohs.

We drove from the airport to the hotel through a world of strangely opalescent orange fog. Preconceived ideas I had about the exotic mystery of the shrouded Middle East appeared to be an actuality. There was a rude awakening at the hotel. This was definitely twentieth century—no mystery here, only the very best of service and modern conveniences. There was certainly nothing sinister about the friendliness of everyone milling about the lobby, or the bell boy's big smile and his "weclum" to Egypt.

The morning light brought with it a hazy sunshine and our first real glimpse of Cairo and its legendary Nile. What a fantastic sight: the Cairo tower rising high above the city and the Nile wending its way as far as the eye could see. We could also see the bustle of the city below, though maybe not as busy as usual because it was Friday, an Islamic holy day.

Cairo is a city of 11 million, a city that was originally built for just 500,000, so you can imagine the excitement and fervor it generates. Language was really no barrier here; nearly everyone seemed to speak some English and/or French and even Italian, perhaps due to the influx of tourists through the years.

We took it as a sign of their willingness to please that the native Egyptians would bother to learn these languages. Reading Arabic is something else again; however, many signs were also in English, so getting around was not quite as hazardous as one might think. We were fortunate to have people there that took special care of us, who went out of their way to make us feel at home, and for this we are truly indebted to them.

For me "Egypt" has always conjured up visions of pyramids, sphinxes (is there a plural for *sphinx?*), bazaars, endless expanses of sand, and the magic of the Nile. I was not disappointed; it was all this and more.

The blending of the old and the new, Christianity, Coptic, and Islamic, is exotic, oriental; it is both ancient and modern and it casts its own peculiar spell over the visitor. You might yet still glimpse the classic features of the ancient Egyptians in the faces of the people. These were the Coptics, or Christians, and with the influx of Bedouins and those from the south came the Islams, creating a perfect blend of religion and race.

The color and excitement of Cairo certainly gets the old adrenaline flowing. You feel so alive and aware—actually you need to be on your toes in Cairo, for to cross the street safely you need all the awareness you can muster. It is a perpetual game of "chicken." I came away convinced that drivers in Cairo are equipped with some form of personal radar, how else could they possibly maneuver through streets made for two lanes and handling four or five?

Surprisingly there seems to be few accidents—prayer beads are essential. It is one of the most amazing feats I have ever witnessed, this ability to move in a veritable sea of automobiles with no apparent guidelines. We were advised that in Cairo, one needs a small car with a large horn. Certainly the cacophony of horns is part and parcel of the sights and sounds of modern Cairo.

Most of us when we think of the Nile think of the mysterious river—we see Cleopatra, Mark Antony, and Caesar. In actuality the Nile is the very heart of Egypt. The land along its banks is extremely fertile and beautiful. One never quite gets used to seeing the contrast of oceans of sand and the green, green fertile areas along the Nile and where the land has been reclaimed through irrigation. There is a lot of sugar cane grown along the Nile. A not unusual sight is a young boy trotting along on his donkey enjoying his "stick" of sugar cane. Alfalfa is grown to feed the donkeys, horses and bullocks, and the goats. Immense cabbages and cauliflowers and all kinds of vegetables and fruits are also grown. Especially delicious are the madarins, and, of course, dates. I found it just as I had pictured it in my mind: the desert, the green oasis with the palm trees, and the blue skies—I was not disappointed.

We saw women washing their pots on the banks of the Nile, bullocks and goats and sheep being driven along the dusty streets. We saw women carrying anything you might imagine on their heads. We saw beautiful dark-eyed children, always with the charming grin. We saw laden donkeys and camels—scenes from Biblical times that still have their rightful place in the twentieth century. Constantly we noticed the contrast between the old and the new. The big modern hotels and office buildings sit side by side with the beautiful mosques and street bazaars. At intervals throughout the day we heard the call to prayer, an important part of the citizens' daily lives.

Our friends took us to a street bazaar where you could get a great deal on a camel saddle or on other exquisite and abundant handicrafts. Joe was in seventh heaven; he loves to barter. We had a little difficulty in dragging him away, but everyone had a great time. The children especially liked to practice their English on the tourists—"No charge to look" they cried with that infectious grin. Who could say no?

We visited an Egyptian pancake house that was similar to a pizza place. You were able to observe the performance of the chef. He took a round of dough, almost like a puff pasty, and gradually made it larger and larger and flatter and flatter, then he spread it out on oiled marble and we picked out our choice of fillings—meats or sweets. This he put inside and folded the dough over. Next he threw our "pancake" into a large concave pan over a very hot open fire. The pancake puffed up immediately and in minutes we were enjoying this delicious hot concoction. We also visited a small, family-run restaurant in the bazaar, where we had the best Kafka kabob ever. Again, we noticed that everything was cooked over hot, open fires.

One evening we had dinner (yes, we did eat a lot!) in a "tent." It was a restaurant set up to resemble a bazaar, with a buffet of all the best Egyptian foods imaginable. The pita bread was cooked "the old-fashioned way" in a small, very hot oven, and was eaten while still hot and steaming. We were introduced to some excellent Egyptian cuisine. The desserts were certainly not for weight watchers. There were many and varied delicious puddings, and my favorite, a type of baklava made from a finely shredded dough and filled with nuts and honey. We also sampled a terrific sherbert made from *Kakadei*, which are dried flowers. These are seeped for a while and they can be used for a hot or cold drink, or as a sherbert. It is purported to be good for high blood pressure, so I would imagine that the automobile drivers in Cairo drink great quantities of this!

Egyptian cuisine is a little hard to define. It is really a combination of several Mediterranean cuisines: Lebanese, Turkish, Greek, Syrian, and Palestinian. The methods of cooking vary, as do some of the basic ingredients because of the locale. The vegetables and fruits are usually locally grown and sold fresh. All beverages are nonalcoholic, although they do serve a good Egyptian beer and they do produce some wine. Of these beverages we preferred the *Omar Khayam*.

Our next stop was Luxor, located south of Cairo, a beautiful resort renowned for its dry air and clear skies. In the western hills of Luxor lies the Valley of the Kings and Queens. This is the location of the tomb of Tut-Ankh-Amun, and also those of Ramses III, Ramses VI, and Ramses IX, among others—Ramses was a very popular name. The tombs are truly magnificent. Their hieroglyphics have maintained their colors and looked as though they had been carved just that year. Probably the most interesting, albeit the smallest, was the tomb of King Tutankhamen. The frescoes in the funerary chamber were splendid, as were the treasures that were found there, most of which are now in the Museum in Cairo, another must on a visitor's list. The very idea that everything was left in these tombs so that the deceased might have all his needs for his new life is just fascinating, and the more you see and listen, the more you believe. This is one phase of ancient Egypt where I honestly believe one could spend hours and hours and still want to know more. Also at Luxor is the Karnak Temple. The best way to see this is at night at the Sound and Light show and as the pyramids and Great Sphinx in Cairo are shown.

The Karnak Temple is unbelievable. In stature alone it is the most impressive sight I have ever seen, although the pyramids are just as impressive. The beautiful statuary in Rome and Greece are like miniatures compared to the immense works one finds here. This is where the pharaohs walked and talked, and the feeling is one of grandeur and golden days and an unexcelled dynasty. I personally would have loved to have walked alone there at night, to hear the echo of the voices and to be transported back in time.

Next, we felt it was time to go the regular tourist route and sit on a camel to have our pictures taken. Well, our camel drivers had a better idea: Go for a short ride! The initial step in getting on the camel is not too bad, but when it starts to get up, things get a little hairy to say the least—you are sure you are going to sail right over its head. "No, No," the driver said with a smile, "just lean back." Well, riding along is not so bad either, although I would imagine that after riding for any length of time one might be prone to seasickness. Getting off the camel is all the procedure of getting on in reverse. However, it was another new experience, and I wouldn't have missed it for the world. Joe was not too enthusiastic about the smell, but I wasn't affected, maybe because I stayed away from the camel's "rear." Camels are of a notoriously grumpy disposition. In England we have an old adage—when someone is in ill humor, we say they "have the hump." I'm sure I now know where it originated. Apart from all this, though, I really thought camels had a charm all their own, and they do have the loveliest long eyelashes I've ever seen.

In Luxor we visited the Luxor Hotel School. At this time, it had been in operation for two years and was in the process of erecting a hotel that would utilize the skills of the students. The school was a pleasant surprise. The school had large, airy kitchens and classrooms, sixteen students to a class, and two students to a range. At this time there was a dire need for qualified personnel in the hotels in Egypt, and at this school they were training young people to fill this need. The school showed a very promising beginning. The students were enthusiastic and capable, showed interest, and most spoke English quite well.

The questions they asked were pertinent ones, and it was a pleasure to see how concerned they were to acquire more knowledge and skill. We were served an excellent luncheon at the school. The staff were very friendly and helpful. All in all it was a most rewarding experience, especially for Joe because he felt he was able to motivate the young people in the profession.

In Luxor, to get to the West Bank of the Nile one must take a ferry. On the trip across you pass the Feluquas, the fishing boats with their big, rather strange-looking sails, and other ferry boats of indeterminate age and origin. Colorfully garbed merchants come aboard to sell their wares, and seem to enjoy the bargaining as much as their customers do. It is a fun way of doing business. Then there are the shoeshine "boys." I use the term "boys" loosely. Business is booming in the trade because shoes are always dusty and sandy. One of my favorite recollections is of the shoeshine "boy" who took care of Joe. Attached to his shoe box was a bicycle bell. When it was time for his customer to change feet he rang the bell, and woe betide those who were not paying attention. But he gave a great shine, and very inexpensively.

We were driven along the desert road to Ismailia, on the Suez Canal. It is one of the most beautiful areas in all of Egypt. This is where the Middle East Department for Tourism and Hotel Investments, under the direction of Mr. Bahie Eldin Nasr and Mr. Abdel Rahman Selim, was building up a beautiful resort area. To complement this they were in the process of erecting an institution for training in the culinary arts and hotel management. The project was due for completion in March 1985. The resort was located on Alligator Lake, a freshwater lake backing onto the Suez Canal. Consequently, the fishermen, and there were many, had a choice of freshwater fish from the lake or saltwater fish from the area where the Suez seeps in. There was almost an optical illusion to behold here: From a distance, the ships sailing up and down the Suez Canal appeared to be sailing atop the sands. This resort in Ismailia seemed to be a great getaway spot for Cairo residents, away from all the hustle and bustle.

The kitchen had very limited equipment and a lack of ingredients. Not to be intimidated, Joe improvised using his hands—and his brains—and came up with some of the best rolls I have ever tasted, a loaf of Alligator bread (for Alligator Lake), and some delicious cream puffs. I believe everyone, including myself, was amazed at what could be accomplished with a minimum of equipment and ingredients and a maximum of ingenuity. We all enjoyed the breads and dessert, and the chef prepared some excellent Egyptian cuisine.

We also enjoyed some of Mr. Nasr's special Jasmine tea. We left Ismailia with the feeling that great things were in store there for the future. Mr. Nasr and Mr. Selim were very enthusiastic about the project and deserved our compliments on their foresight.

By now, my readers are thinking, well, this is all very nice, but if you go to Egypt you should see at least one belly dancer. Oh, we did, quite a few. The last time was on our last night in Cairo. Our very good friends, Mohamad Riad, Bahigu El-Haggar, and Karim Ibrahim, took us on the *Nile Pharoah,* a ship specially equipped to resemble a pharoah's barge, to sail on the Nile while enjoying a sumptuous dinner, prepared by a chef who had attended Joe's seminar. He was so excited to see us there, and so honored. He did a great job on the food. The dancer did a great job with her "belly" and all in all it was a real fun evening.

There was really so much more to the trip that it can't all be told. I could not end here, however, without describing one of the most beautiful and exciting events we have ever witnessed: a traditional Egyptian wedding—don't miss it if you have the chance! They held one almost every night from our hotel (lots of weddings there). The first time we saw one we were in awe. The stairway was decorated with flowers. The guests arrived and it was like a high-couture fashion show—what absolute splendor! Then the throbbing music began, and so did the procession: the trumpeters, the tambourines, the drums. Then the male dancers came forth, whirling and chanting, followed by incense holders and young virgins holding lighted candles. Then the female dancers, wearing headdresses of real lit candelabras, and the belly dancers showed their skills. Finally, the bride and groom entered. As always, the bride was beautiful, in a gorgeous traditional white wedding gown; the groom wore a formal tuxedo. The onlookers threw flower petals and imitation gold coins—which are supposed to be lucky, so we gathered up quite a few. Women showed their approval by "singing" a shrill sound made with their hand on their mouth. This "singing" was also performed in the harems of old, when the wives sat upstairs and looked down through elaborate latticed windows on the men and the entertainment below. Throughout the long wedding procession we heard that continuous, throbbing, happy music. As a matter of fact, it began to be rather a joke with Joe and our friends that I had to get back to the hotel for the next wedding!

We shall not soon forget our trip to Egypt or forget the good friends that we made there—Karim Ibrahim, Bahiga El-Haggar, Mohamad Riad, Mr. Bahie Nasr, and Mr. Abdel Selim. It was an unforgettable experience. The land of the pharoahs and the sacred Nile, was, for us, a land of many wonders both old and new, a trip into the glorious past and the exciting future.

A typical Egyptian menu would consist of the following:

> Rice pilaf or rice nutty pilaf
> Macaroni with red sauce and garlic
> Vegetables in red sauce
> Fried meat and chicken or chicken with béchamel sauce
>
>   or
>
> Meat in white or brown sauce
> Salads (greens with onion and pepper with tihina sauce)
> Pickled eggplant and garlic, turnips in vinegar
> Dessert: Baklava or apricot pudding or milk pudding (all desserts with nuts)

Salatet Tihina
(Tihina Sauce for Salads)
(2 servings)

Ingredients

1 c.	Tihina (oil of sesame seed)
1–2 c.	Water
2 tbs.	Lemon juice
1 tbs.	Vinegar
1/2 tsp.	Cumin
	Salt (to taste)

Optional

1	Small grated onion
3–5	Crushed garlic cloves
	Parsley (to taste)

Method

1. Add water, cumin, lemon juice, salt, and vinegar to tihini and stir thoroughly until well blended and a smooth paste is obtained.
2. Add cumin, lemon juice, vinegar; stir. Gradually add tihina.
3. Add any or all optional ingredients.
4. One can also use a blender at very low speed.

Saniyet Konafa Bil Mokassarat
(Konafa with Mixed Nuts)

Ingredients

1/2 kg	Konafa (dry, thread-like pastry)
1 1/2 c.	Butter
2 c.	Sugar syrup (sugar, water, lemon juice)
1 c.	Mixed nuts (crushed very fine and mixed with sugar)
2 tbs.	Raisins
1 tbs.	Mixed spice

Method

For this recipe two shallow oven trays are needed.

1. Place Konafa in pot over very low fire, add 1 c. of butter and stir with two wooden spoons.
2. Keep lifting Konafa to prevent sticking. Allow plenty of air and butter to penetrate.
3. Lightly fry the raisins until they puff, add the mixed nuts and mixed spice.
4. Line bottom of greased tray with a thin layer of Konafa.
5. Spread nut mixture evenly over Konafa, then cover with the rest.
6. With wet palm of hand, press down.
7. Melt remaining butter and pour over tray, reserving half the amount.
8. Place in center of low oven and cook, allowing top to brown.
9. Turn over into other tray, pour rest of butter and over tray, reserving half the amount.
10. Place in center of low (250°F) oven and cook, allowing top to brown.
11. Turn over into other tray, sprinkle with rest of butter and return to oven, thus browning both sides.
12. Remove from oven and saturate with cold sugar syrup.

Mihallabiya
(Milk Pudding)

Ingredients

3 c.	Milk
3 tbs.	Ground rice
1 c.	Sugar
1 tbs.	Rose water
2 tbs.	Mixed nuts

Method

1. Add ground rice to 1 c. milk.
2. Dissolve sugar in remaining milk and bring to boil.
3. Add rice-milk mixture, lower heat and cook, stirring occasionally, until pudding thickens like thin custard.
4. Remove from fire, stir in rose water and pour into shallow serving dish.
5. Sprinkle top with nuts.

Kossa Abaama
(Stuffed Zucchini)
(2 servings)

Ingredients

1	Small zucchini
1/2 kg	Savory beef (minced beef, onions, salt and pepper)
1–2 tbs.	Pine nuts (optional)
3 c.	Yogurt
1–2	Egg whites
	Salt and pepper (to taste)

Method

1. Core zucchini.
2. Add pine nuts to minced beef and stuff zucchini loosely.
3. Place in pot, add enough water to barely cover and boil for 10 min.
4. Stir egg whites into yogurt and pass through wire sieve onto cooking zucchini.
5. Add seasoning and cook uncovered for 15–20 min.

Reader's Notes and Thoughts

Joe Amendola and Chef Peter Berini preparing for a continuing education presentation at the Culinary Institute of America.

What a Wonderful Profession

During the early years of my employment at the CIA the school would operate from September to June and close in the summer months, as did all other academic institutions. It wasn't until years later that the school calendar went year round, keeping faculty and students on campus through the hot summer months.

The students would get a chance to practice what they learned in class in local restaurants and bakeries when the school was closed, and the chef instructors would go to work at summer resorts and hotels throughout the country to keep their edge on what was happening in the culinary scene. Ironically, the school closing in the summer gave all of us additional opportunities to learn, and I was no exception.

I chose to go to work during my summer vacations with Chef Jones as a pastry chef at the Wequassett Inn at Chatham Mass in Cape Cod. Although it was not close to New Haven, it was worth the trip; the reputation of the resort promised to give me great opportunities to refine my craft and learn from other seasoned professionals. I've always loved learning new things, and the work at the inn was more fun and exciting to me than I could have ever imagined at the time.

Why did I say "what a wonderful profession"? The culinary and hospitality industries offer many great opportunities for young and practiced professionals—from cook and chef to educator, owner, and consultant. There are many jobs and many different career paths for people to choose from. There's something for everyone no matter what your personal strengths and ambitions may be.

Also, it is the people you get to meet in this profession that no other profession can rival. I have met U.S. presidents and political leaders from around the world; I've met army generals and navy admirals from America, Britain, and Japan; and I've met more than my share of the world's greatest chefs in the twentieth century, including Paul Bocuse and Roger Vergé, who both visited the CIA in later years. It all started with my army experience and then continued with my various posts at the CIA; and it is not over yet. In February 2005, I will be traveling to Brazil to continue to meet and greet rich, famous, and powerful people with whom I hope to build close relationships and friendships.

It was only a two-and-a-half-month assignment, back in 1948, when as an instructor at the New Haven Restaurant Institute I took a summer job at the Wequassett Inn from Memorial Day to Labor Day. I recall that we were given a cottage so that our families could come and stay with us because we worked seven days a week and for long hours each day. It was too much and too long for anyone to commute very far from the Cape, but it was also good for families to stay together. My wife Marjorie and our children (Jeannie and Joey) could go to the beach every day during those hot summer months, and I went to the kitchens. I did this for several summers.

Early in the 1960s Mrs. Roth decided that not only students needed summer training, but also the working cooks and chefs who could not take off from work to attend a full-time school program needed professional development as well. Many of them had no formal education, and though they were practiced in their craft, they could all benefit from refined and proper training. So, some of our instructors were retained year round in their teaching positions, and the CIA and Mrs. Roth started a summer refresher program for experienced cooks and chefs.

In the first year Chef Louie Bartenbach, Chef Arthur Jones, Chef Leroi Folsom and I were assigned to this new program. We also invited

Wequassett Inn, Chatham, Massachusetts

some renowned chefs such as Pierre Berard, Joseph Donon, and Richard Bosnjak from Cornell University as guest instructors, to name a few.

In future years we began to take our refresher cooking team to other large cities like Chicago and Boston so that chefs from that area would not have to travel to New Haven to get the education and training they sought.

A great part of this endeavor was that we all learned from one another. At times it was hard to tell who the students were and who the teachers were. Everyone had something to contribute to the learning process, and we were encouraged to listen to what everyone had to say about the unique ways they cooked and baked foods to compare and contrast it with what we were teaching at the Institute. It was a perfect way to spread the reputation of the Institute, and keep its curriculum on track for producing graduates with the proper skills and knowledge to succeed in the growing business of hospitality and foodservice.

On occasion, we would invite chefs such as Herman Rusche from the famous Greenbrier Hotel and Resort in White Sulfur Springs, West Virginia; Casey Sinkeldam, a well-known pastry chef and member of 1966 ACF Culinary Olympic team; and Henry Haller, who was chef at the White House and a great friend for many years. The refresher program allowed us to network with great chefs around America and around the world, learning and sharing our knowledge and expertise with each other.

This program has continued to grow to become a great asset to CIA and is now known as CIA's Continuing Education Program, housed in a beautiful building on its Hyde Park campus and also the Greystone campus in Napa Valley, California.

During my tenure at the Culinary Institute of America I was blessed to be able to develop a world full of great friends. Besides the great alumni, over 25,000 by the time I retired, many of whom have since created their own great careers, and over 250 cooking and pastry instructors I had the opportunity to work with, I was able to make friends with many of the industry's greatest business leaders. I've had the pleasure of meeting and calling friend the following industry greats: Bill Marriott, Charles Forte, Peter Grace, Baron Hilton, and Malcolm Forbes. Also included on my list of friends are Joe Baum, the great restaurateur; Massimo Ferrari from Brazil; Luigi Laverini, whom I met for the first time in London, England; Mr. Takaki and Tonaka from Japan; Sergio Lorenzi from Pisa, Italy; Ma Gi from China; Jimmy Wu (it was and still is common practice for many Asian businesspeople to take on an English-sounding name so they can conduct business around the world) from Hong Kong; and Mr. Narula from India.

Many of the school's accomplished alumni still keep in touch with me even though they are consumed by their own business and reputations. I asked a few of them to say a little something of our times together. Enjoy what they had to say, as I will cherish their words for the rest of my days.

I met Joe Amendola in 1974, during my first year as a student at the CIA, in the early days of Hyde Park. The school back then was small, but there were some larger-than-life characters . . . like Chef Amendola (and Sonnenschmit, Zach, Elmer, Almquist, etc.), who made the place feel very special. His passion for baking, his dedication to the school and its students, and his gentle and kind demeanor made him a role model for many students. Joe was a gentleman and the kind of chef that makes us all proud of our profession.

Jasper White
Summer Shack Restaurant

On a dreary and wet spring day in 1963, I was on a student-escorted tour of the Culinary Institute of America. Flanked by the ivy-covered Yale University Forestry School and the imposing Divinity School, the Culinary Institute's campus—made up of former mansions of New Haven's elite—was a fascinating and in some ways anachronistic sight. But it was not the architecture that left the biggest impression. Rather, the demeanor and attire of the chef instructors remain etched in my mind. Tall white toques perched high on heads held high, stiff white jackets, and crisply ironed black and white checked trousers set both a sartorial and exacting stage. Then we were escorted into the bakeshop. Surprisingly, the four gentleman holding court wore almost shapeless toques and white short-sleeved shirts as they casually addressed the students. By comparison the bakeshop seemed less regal. However, I was not aware that it reflected the personality of the man in charge, head bakeshop instructor "Joe" Amendola, a humble, but fiercely determined man who would at one point in his long and distinguished career lead the school as interim president. Mr. Amendola, as he was then addressed, rather than Chef Amendola, did not teach or lead via attire, titles, or other formalities. Instead his enthusiasm, friendliness, professionalism, and passion for baking provided a measure of direction that helped set more culinarians on the road to success than one could possibly imagine.

Marcel Desaulniers
The Trellis, Williamsburg Virginia
Author: *Death by Chocolate*

I go back with Joe to the CIA in New Haven, 1963–1965, when he was an instructor and I was a student. *The Baker's Manual* by Joe Amendola, which has seen its days of practical use, sits on my book shelf for anyone to borrow. This book more so than any other book in my collection has more tattered pages and more scotch tape holding it together because it has found its way into many more hands then mine because of the basic teachings of the book and Joe's writings of the foundation he taught about baking.

My understanding of baking has come from Joe's teaching and his sharing of those basics in 'The Baker's Manual'. More far-reaching than the knowledge he has imparted on the subject of baking has been the understanding I have gained from watching Joe interface with people from our industry. I have been in Joe's presence many many times as he portrays "The Ambassador of the Foodservice Industry and the Culinary Institute of America" role. I have greatly appreciated Joe for "the Gentleman and the Gentle Man" he is. Who is to say just how many young culinarians Joe has affected. I for one know and appreciate the effect he has had on my career.

Rod Stoner
Vice President of a Food and Beverage
the Greenbrier Hotel

Few chefs have influenced me in a way that Joe Amendola has, not only during my time at the Culinary Institute of America but also during the years after. As an administrator, Joe played many important roles at the CIA, infusing the culinary arts into our curriculum and also giving us a real grasp of the reality of the restaurant business. He has been instrumental in my work and the work of so many others, and is a true icon in this industry.

Best regards,

Charlie Palmer
The Charlie Palmer Group

I recall the first day at school when all the new students were assembled in Roth Hall, the main CIA building. It was the spring of 1973, and I was among the new class.

Joe stood up and pretty much started to read us the riot act. Having just gotten out of the Navy myself I had been there and done that and had the t-shirt to prove it, but these other rookies were scared to death. Joe was putting the fear of God in them. There was no doubt in anyone's mind that if you messed up you were out of the program, no ifs, ands, or buts. Joe could have been a drill sergeant for the Marines the way he dictated the CIA's dress codes and rules of conduct to us. I remember Joe saying that if anyone didn't like what they were hearing that they had better leave now, on the spot, and save themselves and the CIA a lot of time and trouble. And as if that was not enough, Joe told us that in five years, seven out of ten of us sitting there would not be in the foodservice business. Wow, Joe's statements made us wonder whether or not we had made the right decision to go to the school, but now I know he was right. Thank you Mr. A for being you! It has made me a better chef and a better person.

Sincerely,

Van Atkins, class of 1974
Sr. Director of Business Development
Custom Culinary

When the words *hospitality* and *networking* come to mind, Joe Amendola's picture is there. Having been with Joe in a wide array of settings, there is ALWAYS a line of people waiting to talk to this wonderful human being. With my position I have met thousands of people in our industry, and without question the most respected and appreciated representative of the hospitality industry is Joe. Yet you wouldn't know that when you speak to him, you are as important as anyone else he knows. I am honored just to have him know who I am.

Ed Manley, MCFE, CHM, CPFM
President and Chief Operating Officer
International Food Service Executives Association
and Military Hospitality Alliance

Poppy Seed Filling

Method	(Batch) lb.	oz.	Ingredients
Soak for 6 to 8 hours. Then drain off water and grind poppy seed fine.	4 2		Poppy seeds Hot water
Bring just to a boil. Add to drained and ground poppy seed:	2 4	8 4	Water Honey Granulated sugar Shortening or margarine
Add and mix smooth, increasing cake crumbs or adding egg white to secure desired consistency:	4 4	2 3/4 1/4 12	Cinnamon Granulated sugar Cake crumbs (variable)* Grated lemon rind Salt Whole eggs Egg whites (variable)*
Total Weight	17	11	(283 oz.)

*To reach a thick but fluid consistency.

Cinnamon Cream Filling

Method	(Batch) lb.	oz.	Ingredients
Cream to medium lightness:	5		Powdered sugar
	2	8	Shortening
		8	Cake flour
		8	Cinnamon (variable)
		2	Cocoa
Then add slowly and mix smooth:	1	8	Egg whites
Total Weight:	10	2	(162 oz.)

Chopped Peanut Filling
(For Pastries)

Method	(Batch) lb.	oz.	Ingredients
Mix together:	8		Granulated sugar
	8		Chopped peanuts
Total Weight:	16	(256 oz.)	

Cinnamon Paste Filling

Method	(Batch) lb.	oz.	Ingredients
Mix smooth:	4	8	Powdered sugar
		8	Shortening
		9	Cake flour
		10	Cinnamon (variable)
Then add slowly and mix smooth:	3	8	Vegetable oil
Total Weight:	9	11	(155 oz.)

Reader's Notes and Thoughts

Sorry! My Battery Just Went Dead. He is not trying to make himself look like Clark Gable—this gesture with both hands placed behind both ears, pushing the ears forward indicates hard of hearing, or "simply trying to hear your partner at a disco!" (From Joe Amendola's book *More Than Words Can Express*, unpublished)

American Culinary Federation:
Experience in Networking

I have been a member of the American Culinary Federation (ACF) for over forty years now, and have never doubted the importance of joining and participating in the national federation of cooks and chefs even once. I can't even remember all the many opportunities my membership afforded me to meet great people and chefs from all over the world, and to share the love of my profession, food, and drink with them.

Through my experiences with the ACF I have traveled the world including Japan, China, Egypt, Israel, Brazil, Russia, and innumerable trips to Europe, the Caribbean, and South America. My ACF membership was the perfect balance to my career at the Culinary Institute of America; at the CIA I was helping to shape the lives of thousands of young culinarians and through the ACF my career was helped along by hundreds if not thousands of friends I now have from chef's associations in dozens of other countries including Germany, Italy, France, Great Britain, and Canada.

One clear example of this reciprocity happened when I had the opportunity to assist then-ACF president Keith Keogh, also team manager of the ACF Culinary Olympic Team (1990–1996), to bring a delegation of American chefs to Hong Kong for a culinary tour of unequaled perspective. There we were, the U.S. Culinary Olympic Team, along with Hans Bushkens and other chef friends from WACS (World Association of Cook's Societies), visiting this foreign country under the auspices of global food and hospitality.

Marge and I had already visited China in 1983, and had previously established friendships that helped to open doors and make introductions for this new group of culinary professionals. We were treated with the highest level of respect, which was the greatest complement they could give us.

Politics aside, the ACF and WACS delegation was welcomed with open arms and the greatest dose of hospitality I had ever witnessed. We were treated better than kings; it was as though food and the social aspects that relate to eating and dining in the Chinese culture superceded any other differences, both sublime and obvious.

We traveled throughout the southern regions of China, spending most of our time in the capital city of Hong Kong, but we also canvassed the beautiful, lush countryside that surrounded us. With mountains in the background everywhere we turned, and deep green fields and tall trees all around us, it was easy to get caught up in the beauty and serenity of that ancient country. It was hard to image, so fertile and natural was the land around us, that we were walking along roads and trails that had been used for thousands of years. The Chinese, for all we as Westerners might think of their politics and social challenges, were tenaciously proud of the land that supported them and supplied their bounty of food and other resources.

We ate and dined like princes traveling in a royal caravan. Yet we were only cooks, chefs, and educators with no power or authority other than the command we all shared over cooking and baking. When we were seated at the table our differences seemed to melt away and only the newness of the foods and drinks we tasted told us we were in a foreign place.

The result of the historical visit, where many new friends were made, was a full-length video of professional Chinese chefs preparing and serving the authentic delicacies that adorned our dining tables. The video was excellently produced and detailed every aspect of the cuisine we were so graciously provided.

I brought the video back home with me and made copies for the ACF and the CIA. This allowed friends, associates, and students to have a small taste of what we experienced. The video was expertly produced, and still waits in libraries from New York to St. Augustine for the next student or practiced culinarian to bring the lessons back to life.

Neither the ACF nor the CIA could have imagined the fine gift of learning that we were given as part of our memorable visit. It would have cost us thousands of dollars to do the same ourselves, and the Chinese produced the video with pride, which has an even higher value. It cost us nothing but friendship, but we continue to reap its benefits to this day.

On another occasion I arranged a trip to Brazil for the ACF Culinary Olympic Team for a similar delegation of American chefs to visit that country and explore its food and countryside. This trip also occurred under Chef Keogh's ACF presidency, and likewise was full of excitement, good food, and even greater hospitality.

Another of our trips was to Russia. You must imagine that we were probably the first delegation of American chefs to descend upon the Russian lands, at that time recently released from the grasp of the powerful Soviet Union, which had previously been dissolved. Yet again, we were sheltered from the politics that plague international relationships and afforded the highest forms of hospitality and courtesy.

Becoming and staying active in a professional organization like the ACF, and especially with its international ties to WACS, has created the most extraordinary experiences of my career. I am eternally grateful to the people in the ACF who have helped me in my career, and whom I hope I have helped in return. Following is a small list of some of the accolades bestowed upon me for my willingness to learn and share among culinarians everywhere.

ACF Central Florida Chapter Scholarship Chair (1972–1986)
ACF National Senior Chefs Chair (1996–2000)
Member of the American Academy of Chefs
Culinary Competition Judge
National Ice Carving Competition Judge
Diplomat National Restaurant Association Educational Institute (1985)
ACF American Academy of Chefs Hall of Fame (1992)
ACF Central Florida Chapter Culinarian of the Year (1993)
ACF Southeast Region Chef's Professionalism Award (1995)
Johnson & Wales University Distinguished Visiting Chef (1995)
Lt. John D Mclanghlin Award (1999)
ACF National Chef of the Year Award (2002)
The Herman Rusche Lifetime Achievement Award (2003)
Honorary Member Societé Culinaire Philanthropique International
Food Societies

ASSOCIATION MEMBERSHIPS

American Culinary Federation since 1965
Escoffier Society; Chapter President (1968–1970)
ACF/Central Florida Chef's Association (1972–present)
National Ice Carving Association
The Order of the Golden Toque; Director (1982–1986)
The Antoine Carême Association
American Society of Bakery Engineers
Herman Brighaupt Award Council on Hotel, Restaurant and
Institutional Education
Honorary Member Kyoto Cooking School, Kyoto, Japan

EXTRACURRICULAR ACTIVITIES

International Culinary and Bakery Judge
National Restaurant Association Judge (1980–1994)
International Ice Carving Judge

AUTHORED PUBLICATIONS

The Baker's Manual, 1960; revised 1992; also published
in Japanese and Chinese

Understanding Baking, 1961; revised 1993
Ice Carving Made Easy, 1962; revised 1994
Professional Baking, 1965
Practical Cooking & Baking for Schools and Institutes, 1971

EDUCATION

University of Massachusetts, Amherst, Massachusetts, 1970
University of New Haven, Bachelor of Science, 1972

Reader's Notes and Thoughts

Joe Amendola in military dress during an IFSEA visit abroad.

Military Adventures with the IFSEA

For close to fifty years I have been an active member of another professional organization, in addition to the memberships I carried in the American Culinary Federation (ACF) and later the Retailer's Bakery Association (RBA). This time the organization I joined to help promote the students, faculty, and the entire school was geared toward restaurant owners and general managers. When I joined the New Haven chapter its name was the Stewards and Catering Association, but that was later changed to its present name, the International Food Service Executives Association (IFSEA).

I can not overstate the importance of joining a professional organization for networking, learning, and sharing knowledge. I joined more than a dozen associations in my day, and became active in the three or four of the largest and most influential of them.

I joined these organizations for two purposes: one, to improve the reputation of the Institute by exposing professional managers, bakers, and cooking chefs to our classrooms, curriculum, faculty, and students, and two, for my own professional development and networking opportunities, on which I have thrived for over half a century.

Eventually these associations brought hundreds if not thousands of potential students to the Institute's doors. Each one of them was, and still is, interested in a long-standing membership, and there was no better time to capture people as potential life-time members than when they begin to climb their career as students or apprentices. It was then and still is today a win-win situation for both the organizations, which are dependent on memberships to run their networks, and for the students, who could mingle and learn from the already successful professional managers, bakers, and chefs in their own area or town. Many of the most prominent people in the industry would be asked to lead discussion groups and/or conduct demonstrations for all those in attendance at the monthly meetings, sharing their skills and knowledge with everyone. I can't think of a better way, outside of the Institute's classrooms, for a young person to meet and greet already successful restaurateurs, chefs, bakers, and pastry chefs on terms that they both can benefit from.

After seventy-five years in the foodservice industry, it would be hard for me to say whether I met more influential people at the CIA or through my active memberships in these professional organizations. Sure, I was lucky to be a part of what has become the country's most well-known culinary college, the CIA, but I would have had great opportunities to meet chefs and restaurateurs from all over the world even if I never entered 393 Prospect Street in New Haven or Roth Hall (the name given to the main building at the CIA on its New York campus in honor of Mrs. Roth, the Institute's founding director) in Hyde Park. In the early years I would just go to the meetings to network and learn from others, and in later years I would be asked to hold those powerful discussion groups and to demonstrate baking and pastry skills to others. Now I can enjoy the memories, the friendships, and the knowledge I gained through my association with those national, even international, organizations.

Let me tell you about some of my experiences working with IFSEA and the many great places I was able to visit, experiences I was able to have, and the many friends I was able to make and keep all these years later through my association with the international organization. If I could do it, so can you.

The International Food Service Executive Association has developed a solid professional relationship with the U.S. Military, especially the army, navy, and marines, for many years now. It seems the military has finally learned that one of the best ways to motivate and train soldiers and sailors is by providing them with healthy, tasty, and nutritious meals. The canned and dehydrated rations that were so important to supply soldiers with needed food in the field were not appropriate for peacetime meals, and far from appropriate for battle meals when hot and cold fresh foods could be made available.

For over fifty years, since the close of World War II, military cooks and bakers have tried to perfect the art of cooking and baking in the field, that is, away from any permanent structures such as normal dining halls and professional kitchens. To do this has required the innovation of many different types of outdoor cooking and holding equipment, similar in design to their professional kitchen cousins, yet fueled by portable heat sources including everything from diesel fuel to propane.

Diesel fuel had been the preferred fuel for years because it was used to run military trucks and other mobile units. That way they only needed to carry one type of fuel for everything. Unfortunately, the petroleum-based fuel left undesirable fumes and tangent flavors for the foods and bakery products baked under its intensive heat.

Propane was also experimented with extensively for it produces a much cleaner and odorless fire; unfortunately the volatility of propane and potential for fire and explosion made it impractical and even unsafe in many battlefield operations. Now, I understand, the military is using a completely different type of fuel for the field cookery units known as APF (all-purpose fuel), which is less volatile than propane and less odorous than diesel. I wish them luck.

To promote the development and service of quality foods to military personnel, IFSEA had a hand in establishing a series of culinary awards that challenged the different bases, mess halls, and galleys to produce high-quality foods in clean and sanitary conditions, even in the most precarious operations.

I was able to put on my camouflaged khakis time and time again, this time as a visiting dignitary and not a sheet-metal specialist, as I visited military bases and ships around the world. I consider that some of my greatest experiences were afforded me when I was assigned to nine different projects as a food excellence award consultant and judge over the past twenty to twenty-five years.

IFSEA has been conducting foodservice excellence award programs for the military since 1957. Beginning with the U.S. Army, now all branches of the military have some kind of foodservice award to showcase the expertise of their cooks and to promote competition among the various branches.

You might be asking, what kind of foodservice does the military provide that could qualify for excellence awards? In retrospect, looking at the beginning of the awards, there probably wasn't much in quality of foodservice that the military could prove competent in. Sanitation, cleanliness, and professional dress of the kitchens and staff were probably the only items on the checklist that the various branches could confidently champion. But what about the quality of food on the plate? What awards would they be eligible for?

I guess you might be surprised, as I have often been, that quality foodservice is possible even in the harsh environments under which many of the military have to operate. No, I'm not talking about grand cuisine, but there have been times when I was impressed by the foods they were serving. We did not have to compromise rigid quality standards because of preconceived inefficiencies in skill and delivery by military personnel; we made awards that reflected the highest standards possible given the environment in which they were met.

I made approximately six military evaluation trips representing the IFSEA and the ACF, including multiple trips with the U.S. Marine Corps, U.S. Navy, and U.S. Army. While doing so, I traveled with the honorary rank of Brigadier General or Rear Admiral.

These trips each lasted three to eight weeks, and covered as many as 100,000 miles. As normal procedure, I was always accompanied by one or two military personnel during my visits.

The military traveler accompanying me would concentrate on military-specific information such as forms, reporting, and financial information. My role, as a civilian chef, was to bring an outside and

Joe Amendola with an army soldier visiting a mobile army battalion group.

unbiased look at the overall operation from a functional standpoint: sanitation, customer satisfaction, decor, attitude, and so on.

When we did visits for the U.S. Navy we would normally visit three ships or bases together in a variety of categories, such as Aircraft Carriers, Small Ships, Large and Small Bases, National Guard—a total of over twenty-five categories. So, for example, navy personnel would pick three aircraft carriers that they felt were the best, and the team would visit each one while deployed at sea to observe them in normal operations. In that way, selecting the best ship would be based on actual performances and not just readiness.

Though the team was not there to teach, as such, I would always be asked to share experiences and provide pointers about how they might improve what they were doing. I always love to talk about cooking and baking and the culinary profession whenever I'm given the opportunity.

Many members of the ACF who are also IFSEA members have enjoyed these experiences as I have. It's still a great way to see the world, share your expertise with others, and learn from them. Perhaps the IFSEA and the ACF should to do more projects like these together; after all it is a big and complex industry we work in, and everyone has a specific role to play. I'm happy I was open-minded enough to participate, and am proud of the experiences I now have.

Here are the award programs the IFSEA has established through the military, and which I had the pleasure of participating in over the years:

- U.S. Army: Philip A. Connelly Awards, established in 1968 to showcase the excellence rating of various dining facilities and small and large field kitchens, including battalion units (their grand size can sometimes be daunting) around the world including the U.S. National Guard and Reserve units.

- U.S. Air Force: The John L. Hennessy Award was the first award, established in 1957 and named for John Hennessy, a hotel and restaurant executive who helped to promote quality foodservice in the military. It is a competition open to single- and multiple-unit facilities as well as the U.S. Air Force Reserves.
- Military Sealift Awards: These awards were established in 1992 to bring into the fold of military competitions the foodservice offered by this elite branch of the U.S. Navy. This series of competitions includes small and large fleet auxiliary force ships.
- The Edward F. Ney Award was established for the U.S. Navy in 1958, just one year after the U.S. Army's award program got started. It was named for the head of the subsistence division of the U.S. Navy during World War II, Captain Edward F. Ney, who championed the cause of getting needed supplies to sailors around the globe's oceans and seas with quality precision. The award is built with some of the same visions of quality and precision that helped America maintain its fight in World War II by having needed supplies when and where they needed them. The Ney Awards are contested in ten different categories because of the wide range of vessels the U.S. Navy employs: small, medium and large ashore bases, submarines, afloat battle vessels, hospital ships, and aircraft carriers
- The W. P. T. Hill Awards have been vied for by the U.S. Marine Corps, wherever they are placed to aid in the protection of the country, since 1971. Named after Quartermaster General William Hill, who held that rank prestigiously from 1944 to 1955, the award is open to competing mess halls, field mess, and reserve field mess operations everywhere.

It's been fun to watch the competition of one branch of the service influence the foodservice of the others. The different branches of the military are naturally competitive with each other, for they fight to reach and maintain recruits from the same group of potential candidates. The military has just as many concerns over employee turnover as do commercial enterprises. The service that can recruit and retain appropriate levels of personnel in each of its special groups can achieve its goals with efficient consistency, and those that can't struggle to do so.

It's hard to describe in words the great experiences I had being airlifted onto U.S. Navy carriers in the middle of the Pacific, visiting onboard submarines, mine sweepers, U.S. Army and Air Force bases, and U.S. Coast Guard cutters. I've flown in air force jets, navy helicopters, and transport planes of all descriptions. I've been driven around in jeeps, trucks, and motorcades, and I even had a ride in a tank one day just for the experience.

When traveling with the U.S. Army I was given the honorary title of General, and when with the U.S. Navy, Admiral, so I could have access to the places and people needed to conduct my investigations. The courtesies that have been shown to me while acting in those roles would be ranked among the highest I have experienced anywhere.

The places I traveled and the people I met fill my mind with memories of good times, great camaraderie, and good food. Money could not buy such an outstanding list of experiences, experiences I hope to continue in the years to come.

When it was all said and done, I was awarded a prestige award called the Order of the Dinner Gong in Hawaii from my friends at the IFSEA. The award may have a strange name, but I was grateful for the acknowledgment it meant for me, for all the work I had done to promote the IFSEA and help improve military foodservice around the world.

Streusel Topping (Plain or Chocolate)

Method	(Batch) lb.	oz.	Ingredients
Cream together:	1		Granulated sugar
	1		Shortening or margarine
		1	Malt syrup
		4	Whole eggs
Mix in carefully until crumbly:	2	4	Cake flour
Total Weight:	4	9 (73 oz.)	

Peanut Butter Streusel

Method	(Batch) lb.	oz.	Ingredients
Cream together:	2	8	Peanut butter
	3		Light brown sugar
	2	4	Shortening
Mix in carefully until crumbly:	6	8	Cake flour
		3/8	Salt
Total Weight:	14	4 3/8	(228 3/8 oz.)

Beehive Topping

Method	(Batch) lb.	oz.	Ingredients
Heat to 220°F:	2		Granulated sugar
Remove from heat.	2	8	Honey
	2		Shortening or margarine
Then add and mix in:	2		Sliced Brazil nuts
Total Weight:	8	8 (136 oz.)	

Goodnight Mrs. Calabash—Wherever you are. Most of us have done this at sometime for a child, showing them it is time to sleep, we pillow the head on the hands, and hope they get the message. (From Joe Amendola's book *More Than Words Can Express*, unpublished)

Takaki

My first visit to Japan to meet Mr. Takaki of the world-famous Takaki/Anderson Baking Company, based in Hiroshima, Japan, was soon to become one of my most exciting and memorable trips. The people I met during my visit there have not faded from my memory, and the friendships I made have lasted all of my life. Marge and I continue to reap benefits from these friendships in ways I never could have guessed.

I was invited by Takaki for a brainstorming session regarding improving their bakery manufacturing processes—baking, of course, being my expertise and processes my passion.

I was greeted at the airport in Tokyo by the Takaki family, and was driven to their main office and boardroom via a large, private limousine. There I was met by other senior company officers including the heads of several departments. Although everyone demonstrated great hospitality and courtesy, I still needed the aid of an interpreter to enable me to conduct a thorough investigation and consultation.

I think what impressed my hosts the most was not my knowledge or vast years of experience, but my willingness to say when I didn't know something. I suppose it was the humbling of my self in their presence that ignited the deep respect and friendships we have enjoyed ever since. I didn't know everything, of course, but I was willing find out and let them know.

At the end of a two-week stay, the remaining question on the table concerned what was new in the American bakery industry that could benefit Takaki and his growing business in Japan and throughout Asia. I asked if they had ever heard of high-quality frozen bread dough that could be thawed out and used as needed. Their eyes opened wide. What magic could allow that to happen? But it wasn't magic; it was just new technology that I was happy to share with my new friends.

I told them of my friend Chester Borck, who had pioneered this new technology in America, and promised to help put together a meeting between Chester and Takaki's representatives on what proved to be a most successful trip set up a few weeks later. They jumped at the chance to send two of their head bakers to the United States to learn this new technology of frozen dough.

When I returned to the United States from Japan I called Chester Borck right away and told him of the plan for a visit from the Japanese bakers to learn about creating the perfect frozen dough, and his reply was, "no way!" At first I was taken aback, but then realized I had only spoken about what the Japanese bakers wanted. When I told Chester that he could help expand his technology throughout Asia and Europe by working with Takaki and his bakers rather than closing doors to them, he understood completely the potential of such an international alliance. Chester then agreed to the visit and he and Takaki have been associates and friends ever since.

Today Takaki/Anderson is one of the leading high-quality frozen bread dough and bakery product manufacturers in the world. Chester Borck, the Takaki family, and I have remained the greatest of friends ever since.

It was my personal association with the Takaki/Anderson Company and friendships with their principal players that made possible the huge donation they made to the Culinary Institute for construction of two advanced baking centers. One would be constructed on its Hyde Park campus and the other in California's Napa Valley, where the Institute's western campus for professional development, Greystone, emerged from the stone walls and ardent fields of an old winery nestled in the warm countryside of the same name. It seemed that buying a winery to continue to grow the CIA's continuing education program, which I had a hand in starting in 1948, was as natural as serving good wine with dinner or as a toast among friends.

Now there are two baking and pastry institutes carrying the name of Takaki/Anderson, where many future generations of cooks, bakers, and pastry chefs can learn and perfect their crafts.

Reader's Notes and Thoughts

No, no, please not that! You can have all my tinker toys. I think maybe he's just seen the Frankenstein monster—or maybe his wife!—he's begging to be let alone, both arms extended, palms out, trying to ward off the attacker. (From Joe Amendola's book *More Than Words Can Express,* unpublished)

A Russian Adventure

A mericans were rarely welcomed into the old Soviet Union because of the political differences that existed between the two countries stemming from World War II. The communistic approach to government, social values, and commerce was so different from the way things are done under a democracy such as the United States that the Soviets thought of American travelers as real threats to their way of living. Americans who did brave a trip to the Russian conglomerate were often met with ridicule, contempt, and strict government scrutiny.

With the break up of the Soviet Union in 1991, everything changed. The iron rule of the Communist Party lost its grip and a new government was forming that seemed open to exchange ideas, notions, and even dreams with other people around the world. Could it be that Soviet Russia and the new Russia could be so similar, yet so different? I'd like to say that I, and about thirty other ACF members, were pioneers there, too, for we braved the new air that was floating over old Soviet soil and waters and planned a culinary tour of Russia. It was our way of making a statement that foodservice and hospitality always have and should remain nonpolitical functions in a global economy.

I had the honor of representing our country as a citizen ambassador on this culinary excursion that took us to the western regions of the former Soviet Union. With me were representatives of eight U.S. culinary schools and colleges, which truly marked it as an educational trip with zero parallels. With another thirty-plus chefs representing everything from private restaurants to exclusive country clubs, the ACF and I were armed for fun, adventure, and, we hoped, great food.

This excursion was coordinated through the International Resource Development of Spokane, Washington, and the Moscow Company for International Exchanges. I was appointed as the delegation's leader because I had been around so long, had already made many successful international trips, and was well acquainted with customs and other international travel worries. The trip went perfectly as planned; the only surprise was the openness and great hospitality of our Russian hosts, which we eagerly accepted.

When in Russia we had the chance to meet with a host of government officials, chefs, hotel and restaurant operators, culinary educators, culinary students, and caterers wherever we traveled throughout the newly reclaimed country. If we hadn't been aware of the recent break up of the Soviet Union we might not have been surprised, but with everything the media had taught us about the differences between our two cultures, when it got down to food the differences melted away.

We traveled to three diverse republics, the Ukraine, Georgia, and Russia, visiting the cities of Kiev, Pyatigorsk, and Moscow, respectively. Food markets were of particular interest to us; we enjoyed comparing the Russian counterpart to what we had become familiar with on other travels and within the United States. We had heard so many stories about the unavailability of food that several members of our group brought along their own snacks packed neatly in their suitcases so they wouldn't go hungry at night.

But this was truly an attitude reflecting fear more than reality. We saw no shortages of food in the Ukraine or southern Russia, at least none affecting us or the people we met there. There were no lines at state food stores as we had seen on American television, although we did see them for imported goods. There might have been empty shelves in the state-run stores, but the farmers' markets were full of goods ready to be sold for the right price. How many people could afford those prices is altogether a different question. Needless to say, the group I was with never experienced a shortage of food or drink (or dance and music).

Appetizers represent a little taste of what we experienced in Russia. Russian appetizers are called *zakuski*. They are featured items of Slavic menus, and were a favorite part of all of our meals. Often, over fifteen items were awaiting us when we sat down to eat. Caviar, smoked salmon, sturgeon, sliced galantines, salamis, breads, pickled and fresh vegetables, and mushrooms started almost every meal, followed by borscht or a hot cream soup, then by a hearty main course. Ice cream (particularly vanilla) was the dessert we found most often, but occasionally there would be a torte or other pastry to sweeten our palates.

Kiev

Arrival into Kiev was like stepping back in time to the 1930s–1940s era when America was engulfed in the Great Depression. Kiev was basically leveled during World War II, during what is now referred to in the Ukraine as the Great Patriotic War of 1939–1945. Kiev's present construction reflected almost totally post-1945 architecture. The only exception was the west bank of the city, where hundreds of new apartments had recently been built for the newly expanding citizenry.

Within a few hours of our arrival in the Ukraine, our group embarked upon a true eating adventure. After checking into the Intourist

Hotel, we were escorted to the Dnieper Dining Room for a memorable meal with new friends, many of whom were Russian chefs and pastry chefs. For appetizers we were served pickled vegetables, sliced duck and plums, a pastry shell filled with sturgeon salad, champagne, wine, and mineral water. This menu was followed by a plate of authentic and delicious chicken Kiev, peas, and fried potatoes (the Russian version of French fries). For dessert, a deliciously rich ice cream was presented with stewed plums and orange slices. The service was gracious and was delivered in a professional manner. This was not the picture that our friends back home and the American media had given us prior to our departure.

The Ukraine is known as "the breadbasket of Europe," and we were all eager to find out why. A short visit to the central marketplace in Kiev gave us part of the answer. We were immediately impressed by the vast amounts of fresh produce, fruits, vegetables, fresh herbs, and meats and poultry that we found literally falling off of carts and tables. Again, there didn't seem to be a shortage of food, but rather a shortage of customers. Apparently the Russian ruble had fallen in value so quickly after the break up of the Soviet Union that the average citizen's salary became a fraction of the value it once was.

Our last evening in Kiev was a gastronomic highlight of Ukrainian cuisine. We were guests at the Khata Karasya National Cuisine Restaurant, which was an old cottage with a thatch roof situated in the center of the Ukrainian National Campground. The building's exterior and interior were a marvelous oak structure; the floors, walls, tables and benches, chairs, and an open-hearth oven in the center of the back wall were also made out of exquisite oak boards. Our dining experience was graced further by music from an authentic Ukrainian band that entertained us all evening.

The tables were pre-set family style upon our arrival. The lavish array of appetizers included smoked sardines, stuffed tomatoes, black olives, light and dark rye and pumpernickel breads, stuffed eggs, and a traditional Ukrainian salad of pickled beets, carrots, peas, and potatoes presented in a crusty croustade. Platters of meats and cheeses, included salami, prosciutto ham, smoked hams, farmer's cheese, and Swiss cheeses. Several varieties of mineral water, vodka, peppered vodka, and red and white wines were offered to us around the table without hesitation.

Our second course was also served family style. Huge bowls heaping with potato pancakes topped with sour cream, cabbage stuffed with corned beef and rice, and potato and beef pirogis were set around the table for everyone to share. We expected dessert next but were surprised when bowls of a beef-based stew were set out before us. Huge, tender chunks of beef with potatoes, vegetables, and pan gravy were deliciously prepared and graciously served.

Almost three hours into the evening we were treated to a lavish torte that topped off the meal. The cake was a black forest–date-nut combination made with three layers of cake. Heavy cream with kirsch and chopped walnuts were blended in between the layers.

This restaurant is a must if you ever have the opportunity to visit Kiev. Menu prices of the restaurants we visited were set for table d'hote menus; first class was 50 rubles, high class was 60 rubles, and deluxe was 70 rubles, representing the classes as set by the Kiev Administration of Restaurants Public Catering. We found a la carte menus listing forty items, but prices were only shown for eight of the items; this meant that on that day the establishment could only obtain the necessary ingredients for those eight specific dishes. The availability changed daily.

The Ukrainians seemed apprehensive of all of the changes the future held for them, but they were also excited about the newfound freedoms they were beginning to experience. Most had lived their entire lives under the Communist Party, and were naturally hesitant and uncertain about the things they used to take for granted every day.

Pyatigorsk

Our next stop was at Pyatigorsk, which is located in the southwestern section of the former Soviet Union along the border of the Republic of Georgia. Pyatigorsk is one of four towns that make up Minerainiye Vodi and is located along the southwestern slopes of Mashuk Mountain of the Caucus ranges. It is a very popular resort because of its natural mineral springs and natural mud baths with reported curative powers offered to local citizens and tourists at assorted health facilities dotting the countryside. The heads of state of the former Soviet Union were often sent to this region of the country for medicinal purposes, and thus it had always been kept up with all of the modern conveniences.

Because Pyatigorsk lies close to the Georgian border, the cuisine of this region reflected both a Caucasian and southern Russian influence. Caucasian cuisine is set up almost entirely with local products. We saw trout from the streams, shashlik (meat, fish, and vegetable kebabs), fresh herbs, lots of marinated foods, blinis, pirogis, and inventive zakuski. We also saw huge vegetables such as radishes the size of turnips and carrots twice their normal size due to the rich volcanic soil they were grown in.

We were treated to a feast of Caucasian cuisine at the famous Kislovodsk Zamok restaurant. The fascinating Zamok Castle Rock is southeast of the town of Kislovodsk, located in a ravine made by the Alikanovaka River. This castle reminds one of the ruins of a medieval castle, and is the setting of a local legend about love and treachery.

Our luncheon included discussion of the Caucasian cuisine and local food products with the chef and representatives of the restaurant. The food in this region of the former Soviet Union was very diverse because of the geographical location of the area. The influxes of the cuisine consisted of Turkish, Iranian, Greek, Middle-Eastern, and southern Russian styles. The uses of eggplant, artichoke, fresh trout, plum tomatoes, red peppers, and Syrian breads were prevalent throughout.

We then visited the famous state winery farm, Beshtau, where we had a chance to tour the winery and taste different types of wines made in the region. The lack of cork, generally not available, had a great influence on the finishing process of these wines, which we considered inferior to what we knew of popular French and California varieties. The bottles were sealed with plastic instead, which had a negative effect on the flavor and body of the final product.

It was in this region that our delegation accomplished its most important task. We had the opportunity to visit the Pyatigorsk Polytechnok Institute, something the educators in the group were waiting for. This visit, one of the most productive of the trip, would show us how our counterparts in Russia delivered culinary education.

The Republic of Georgia is renowned throughout the former Soviet Union for the hospitality of its people, and we were greeted at the door of the school by directors and students dressed in traditional costume. As we entered, each of us had to partake of a piece of bread dipped in salt to remind us of the basic properties of food to sustain life in contrast to the other exotic preparation we were soon going to have. We were each given a rose as a sign of everlasting friendship, and were then escorted to our meeting hall.

There we were served delightful pastries, crepes, and other traditional foods beautifully prepared and presented. Instead of teaching French classical cuisine at the school they concentrated solely on Russian and the other 150 styles of ethnic foods found throughout the old Soviet Union. They expressed a great desire to enter into teacher-and-student exchanges with our schools, and we looked forward to long-term relationships that would benefit both sides.

They let us tour their kitchens and meet and mingle with their students and faculty while they were in the midst of a lesson. Some of our group even rolled up their sleeves to show the young Russians a few of their own learned skills.

A general discussion of the educational process for culinary arts in the former Soviet Union as compared to our educational process and standards in the United States was very stimulating. After about two hours the delegation returned to the hotel while I and five of the other educators stayed behind to continue discussions and plans for culinary faculty and student exchanges.

This was perhaps the most meaningful professional accomplishment of the delegation's visit. The thought of a culinary student exchange was well received by the Soviet officials of the school, who were our guests for dinner that evening and who came prepared with a proposed contract for formal exchanges (they are a very disciplined and aggressive culture; we were all happy to call them friends).

We met again in the morning to outline the proposal for the exchange with the Soviet officials. We left this region with a true sense of accomplishment, for we had agreed to a formal exchange of educators and students to begin in the summer of 1992.

Moscow

Moscow is the capital of the former Soviet Union, and also the capital of the Republic of Russia. It was a metropolis of over 8 million people back in 1991; I'm not sure how big it is now. At that time it was the world's fifth most populous city.

Moscow is the administrative, legislative, economic, educational, and cultural capital of the former Soviet Union. It is the embodiment of the Russian character and of Russian history. Moscow is the center for foreign trade and industry organizations, for finance and banking institutions, and for communications and journalism.

Russian cuisine is similar to that of other Eastern European countries. Moscow restaurants provide a generous sampling of regular cuisine as well as the specialty foods of other former Soviet republics, including Azerbaijani, Armenian, Byelorussian, and many other national cuisines. Our professional itinerary included a meeting at the Moscow Main Administration of Restaurants. We met with leaders and managers of the restaurants representing this administration, as well as specialists from the Food Industry Society and the chief of the Moscow Administration of Public Catering. The representatives of these organizations were all prominent culinarians and authors of culinary books. Our general discussions included an overview of the effects of current food production and distribution systems on culinary industries, a survey of the changing legalities concerning foreign investment and joint ventures in the hospitality industry, and unique attributes of Russian and other national Soviet cuisines, as well as current trends in the culinary arts.

To top off the trip, our delegation was given honorary membership in the Moscow Culinary Association, the equivalent group to the ACF. This association of 2,000 members has its own Museum of Public Catering, in which they have created an exhibit for our delegation and for the ACF. Future visits to Russia by ACF members could provide opportunities to contribute to this exhibit. We were shown historic samples of catering and food-processing equipment, menus of prerevolutionary Moscow restaurants, and ancient Russian recipe books. The Chef's Association signed a letter of intent to participate in the 1996 Culinary Olympics alongside the ACF's national team in Frankfurt, Germany.

We followed up this amazing occurrence with lunch at the 6,000-seat Arbat Restaurant, featuring excellent food and, to our amazement, filet mignon.

We also had the opportunity to visit the only American-Soviet joint-venture restaurant in Moscow, Tren-Mos. This restaurant was owned and operated by the Jeffrey Zeigler family of Trenton, New Jersey, hence the name. Mr. Zeigler's Soviet partner is the former mayor of the city of Moscow. The restaurant was decorated throughout with the flags of our nation's states. It offered American cuisine that was gracefully prepared by the executive chef, who was from France. Mr. Zeigler himself was an entrepreneur, twenty-four years old and full of energy, and was the head of a very prosperous and highly regarded operation. Another Soviet-American joint-venture operation that we visited was the Radisson Slav-janskaya Hotel and Business Center. Frank Kiarc, vice president and general manager of the hotel complex, was our host and provided us with some general insight and Radisson philosophy concerning the complexities of the Soviet-American joint venture. We've all heard of the success of the McDonald's franchise in Moscow, and equally successful have been joint ventures with Pizza Hut, Baskin-Robbins, and the long-time association with PepsiCo.

On this short trip, all involved were proud of what a group of thirty-five culinarians could achieve. The gut-wrenching farewell speech of our Moscow guide will remain with us for the rest of our lives as a reminder that we are lucky to live in a free nation.

The twelve days of knowledge that we gained, along with the experience of a lifetime of witnessing a nation in transition, made this a very satisfying excursion. We will be sure to follow up on our valuable leads, and we hope to greet our gracious Soviet hosts on our shores in the very near future.

The following chefs contributed the details for this story:

- David S. Bearl, CWC, CCE, director of the School of Culinary Arts at ATI Career Institute in Falls Church, Virginia.
- Philip J. Cragg, chef instructor at Atlantic Community College in May's Landing, New Jersey.
- Andrew Iannacchione, CEC, executive chef of the Casino at Lakemont Park in Altoona, Pennsylvania.
- Jerry Kuchinskas, executive chef, food and beverage, of Disney's Yacht and Beach Club Resorts in Lake Buena Vista, Florida.
- Normand P. LeBlanc, Jr., chef instructor at Dean Technical High School in Holyoke, Massachusetts.

The Delegates

Leader: Joseph Amendola, CEPC, CCE, AAC, senior vice president and principal, Fessel International, Orlando, Florida, ACF Central Florida Chapter

Linda J. Arndt, ACF Northwoods de Cuisine of Wisconsin

David S. Bearl, CWC, CCE, ACF Nation's Capital Chapter

Mark S. Broistol, ACF Professional Chefs and Apprentices of Omaha

Robert D. Corliss, Virginia Chef's Assn.

Joseph A Cotelessa, ACF, Cape Cod and the Islands

Philip J. Cragg, the ACF Jersey Shore Chef's Assn.

Gerard J. Donnelly, International Chef's Assn., ACF Big Apple Chapter

Karl L. Dratz, CEC, ACF, Albany Chapter

Paul U. Elbling, AAC, Virginia Chef's Assn.

Margaret M. Grotte, CWC, ACF, Midwest Chef's Society of Minnesota

John J. Hudak, Jr., CWC, ACF, Professional Chefs of Northeast Pennsylvania

Andrew G. Iannacchione, CEC, member at-large

Bobby J. Jackson, CWC, Assn. of Military Chefs, Europe

Edward J. Kaminski, III, ACF Triad Chapter, North Carolina

Jerrold Kuchinskas, ACF Central Florida Chapter

Normand P. LeBlanc, Jr., Pioneer Valley Culinary Assn. (Mass.)

Keith J. McCrea, ACF-Sarasota Bay Chef's Assn., Inc.

Bennett A. Mule, ACF Chicago Chefs of Cuisine, Inc.

Willibald G. Neumann, CEC, CCE, AAC, ACF, Midwest Chef's Society of Minnesota

Robert B. Nichols, CEC, ACF Myrtle Beach Chapter

Frances J. Packard, ACF Columbus Chapter

Clark Raines, ACF Myrtle Beach Chapter

Marcella A. Savage, ACF, Inc., Florida Sun-Coast Cooks and Chef's Assn.

Ken K. Siriphant, CEC, Texas Chef's Assn.

Brenda L. Snorton, ACF, Greater Indianapolis Chapter

Lori A. Swahn, Pocono Professional Chef's Assn. (Pa.)

Johannes G. Verdonkschot, CEC, AAC, Chefs de Cuisine Assn. of St. Louis, Inc.

Marcel Walter, CEPC, AAC, Virginia Chef's Assn.

Bruce C. and Geneva Williams, Maumse Valley Chefs Chapter, ACF (Ohio)

John M. Zappone, ACF Cleveland Chapter, Inc.

Thomas and Norma Zarris, ACF Chicago Chefs of Cuisine, Inc.

✍ *Gumbo Glasnost*

In 1988, John Folse, CEC, AAC, chef/owner of Lafitte's Landing in Donaldsonville, Louisiana, was the first American businessperson to complete the negotiation process to operate a restaurant as a joint venture in Moscow. Serving 4,000 customers in two weeks during the Moscow summit, "Lafitte's Landing East" opened the door to future joint-restaurant ventures between the Soviets and Americans. Later, Folse and the ACF hosted a whirlwind culinary tour of the United States for three Soviet chefs.

My mother-in-law can't make it this weekend! Stretching the hands high above the head and using circular movements in this case is not an upper arm exercise—it indicates exuberance, joy and high spirits. (From Joe Amendola's book *More Than Words Can Express,* unpublished)

Fessel International

Forty plus years after beginning as a part-time bakery instructor at the New Haven Restaurant Institute and then the Culinary Institute of America, I decided it was time to leave the Institute to its new brigade of administrators, directors, and teachers and explore other opportunities for me and my wife Marge. Instead of full retirement, then-president Ferdinand Metz asked me to stay on as a CIA "ambassador for life," which I gratefully accepted.

Upon this semi-retirement from the CIA, my wife and I moved to sunny Florida, where we decided to make a new home in Orlando close to a lot of our friends still working in Disney World, Epcot, and other huge Orlando resorts, clubs, and hotels. In addition, Florida promised my wife and me a new haven (Did you catch the pun? *New Haven*) for us to spend our last years in, protected by the warm sun, cool breezes, and flowing countryside, which in 1988 still reflected Florida's natural charm.

It wasn't long after settling in our new home that I met up with an old friend, Jim Armstrong, who retired as vice president of food and beverage from the Disney World Company a few years earlier. I knew Jim fifty years ago when he worked for the great restaurateur and innovator Joe Baum and Restaurant Associates. We've watched each other's careers grow and expand ever since.

It was probably on a golf course, where Jim and I used to spend a lot of relaxing time, or perhaps over lunch at a club or dinner at his or our house, but I decided to mention to Jim my idea of starting a consulting company with its headquarters in Orlando, which had become a hub for business travelers around the world. Jim knew probably more people than I did with all of his business connections, but had already spent his entire life working hard to achieve his goals. He looked at me a little strange at first and said, "I thought we were retired; I'd rather just play more golf or make a trip to Europe to visit some old friends."

"Well actually Jim," I said to him smiling, "that's exactly what I would like to continue to do too. But if we're playing golf or visiting some friends around the world, let's do so on somebody else's dime and teach them a little of what we have learned all these years."

I guess he agreed because shortly afterwards we were building our first set of plans to begin what has since become Fessel International.

Jim was the one who suggested that we needed to branch out and invite other partners into the company. His first recommendation, Randy Hiatt, was a perfect choice. Randy had been involved in foodservice for over twenty years, working for such giants as Marriott, Walt Disney World, the Grace Restaurant Company, and Restaurant Enterprises.

Soon after contacting Randy and telling him our plan over the phone, he agreed to come out of retirement with only one condition: that he be able to remain in California where he was currently living. We all agreed it would benefit our new company to have multiple offices; it would give the impression that it was a larger and broader company than it would able to prove for years to come. "Then let's look internationally," I suggested.

During many of my trips to Zurich, Switzerland I had the pleasure of making the acquaintance of one of that country's leading restaurant consultants, Charles Fessel. I quickly convinced Randy and Jim to go with me on a trip to Zurich and approach Fessel about joining us in our new adventure. He was also thinking of retiring, but was not willing to give up all his connections, business friends, and associates for the permanent golf course or lounge. There was much more work that could be done together to affect real change in the hospitality industry worldwide. All we needed to do was look for a partner in Asia and our brigade would be set.

Quickly the name of Hiroo Chikaraishi came to everyone's mind as the perfect candidate. Chikaraishi, whom we often called Riki for short, was president of Thomas and Chikaraishi, Inc., one of Japan's leading consulting companies for over eighteen years. Riki had also founded a school in Tokyo, Japan specializing in intensive training courses for working professionals in the thriving hospitality and tourism industry, making him the perfect partner for spearheading corporate training and staff development programs. A trip to Tokyo was planned by Jim and myself, and soon we had all four corners of the globe represented by our new firm.

We borrowed Charles Fessel's name for it has that international sound that is easy to pronounce in multiple languages. *Armstrong* was too American, *Amendola* obviously an Italian name, Riki's full name seemed too hard to remember, and Hiat sounded too much like a hotel name. *Fessel* was the easiest to say, spell, and remember and thus became the company's name. Fessel International has been doing business around the world ever since.

I still go to work every day—yes, seven days a week—to my little office in Orlando with the sign "Fessel International" on its door. I may stay for a few minutes or a few hours, or until Marge calls me up to come home for dinner. It doesn't matter, because I still love what I do. It is a job dreams are made of.

Our clients include restaurant chains and independents, attraction owners, commercial project developers, hotels, state and community colleges, cruise ships, and private clubs. We also assist food manufacturers, commercial lenders, advertising agencies, and trade associations involved in providing products and services to the foodservice industry.

Here's a short list of some of our major clients:

Disneyland, Anaheim, California

MGM Grand, Las Vegas, Nevada

Harvard University, Cambridge, Massachusetts

Paramount Studios, Hollywood, California

Nestlé Food Service, Glendale, California

University of Notre Dame, South Bend, Indiana

American Museum of Natural History, New York, New York

General Mills, Orlando, Florida

Universal Studios, Orlando, Florida

Frito Lay in Plano, Texas

Badis in Rabat, Morocco

Legoland in Windsor, England and Germany

Plaza Flamingo in Cancun, Mexico

Takaki Bakery in Tokyo and Hiroshima, Japan

Well I'm not exactly affluent. Thumb and forefinger movement as shown, indicates a lack of funds or food, he's either broke or hungry, or both! (From Joe Amendola's book *More Than Words Can Express,* unpublished)

What Do Retired Senior Chefs Do?
The Power of Continuous Networking

I want to show readers what my travel schedule looked like in 2004, sixteen years after I retired from the Culinary Institute. That day in 1988 when I stepped down from my position at the CIA I knew I wasn't really retiring but was only beginning another phase in my life. All my experiences led me to this part of my life, and I was not about to stand aside and watch what I had spent a lifetime to build fade away. The places I went, the people I met, and the business I helped to transact for major schools and corporations around the world gave me and my wife Marge invaluable memories and relationships that continue to this day. No, I wasn't going to give up—I was even more determined to make the best of it all and continue with the hospitality, foodservice, and consulting that I had enjoyed all my life.

I know I'm not the only senior chef who keeps a busy schedule. It seems that a lot of us spent so much time working and networking all our lives that we have become consumed by the passion of food and hospitality. I travel for business, yes, but also to keep myself alive and vibrant in my senior years.

I still go to work everyday, but it's a pleasure.

This was my 2004 schedule, which I'm hoping to continue into 2005 and for many more years to come. I have a story with each trip, each involving making new friends and renewing old relationships. Make time for people and see what you can achieve.

DATE	EVENT	PLACE	REASON
January 15–17	1st Coast Tech Institute	St. Augustine, FL	Judging
January 26–28	ACF Show	Atlantic City, NJ	Trade Show
January 29	ProStart Show	Orlando, FL	Judging
February 16–18	Food Innovations	Atlantic City, NJ	Trade Show
March 9	Food Innovations	Virginia Beach, VA	Trade Show
March 13–14	New York Restaurant Show	New York, NY	Trade Show
March 16	Food Innovations	Detroit, MI	Trade Show
March 20–23	Retailers Bakery Association	Orlando, FL	Conference

DATE	EVENT	PLACE	REASON
March 22–24	Food Innovations	Minneapolis, MN	Trade Show
March 28–31	Food Innovations	Atlantic City, NJ	Trade Show
April 6	Food Innovations	Louisville, KY	Trade Show
April 14	Food Innovations	Chicago, IL	Trade Show
April 20	Food Innovations	Lakeland, FL	Trade Show
April 29–May 2	ACF	Atlanta, GA	SE Reg. Conf.
May 5–6	Food Innovations	Columbia, SC	Trade Show
May 10	Food Innovations	Toronto, Canada	Trade Show
May 11–13	Food Innovations	Buffalo, NY	Trade Show
May 18–20	Travels with Massimo Ferrari	New York, NY	Culinary Tour
May 21–24	National Rest	Chicago, IL	Trade Show
May 25–27	Travels with Massimo Ferrari	New England	Culinary Tour
May 28–June 2	Various shows and tour	Toronto & Albany	Shows and Tours
June 3–4	Culinary Institute	Hyde Park, NY	Reunion
June 10	Orlando Culinary	Orlando, FL	Judging
June 11	Les Ames D'Escoffier	Orlando, FL	Dinner
June 13–July 6	Portugal, Spain, and Italy	Europe	Culinary tour
July 11–15	Food Innovations	Pennsylvania	Trade Show
July 16–20	ACF	Orlando, FL	Convention
August 8–10	Cloisters Apprentice	Sea Island, GA	Judging
September 20	Culinary Institute of America	Citrus Cove, FL	Alumni Dinner
September 21	Culinary Institute of America	The Living Seas, FL	Board Meeting
September 21–23	Food Innovations	Indianapolis, IN	Trade Show
October 3–4	Bread Baker's Guild	Atlantic City, NJ	Trade Show
October 14	10th CIA Gala	New York City, NY	Dinner
October 15–16	Culinary Institute of America	Hyde Park, NY	Annual Meeting
October 22–24	Florida Restaurant Association	Orlando, FL	Trade Show
October 25–27	Restaurant News Food Tech	Orlando, FL	Trade Show
October 28	Varda Chocolatiers	Lisbon, NJ	Visit
October 29	Les Ames d'Escoffier	New York, NY	Dinner
November 9	21 Club, Wildlife Trust	New York, NY	Reception
November 13–16	I.H.M. and R.S.	New York, NY	Trade Show
Dec. 25–Jan. 1	Christmas and New Years	Orlando, FL	with Marge

Reader's Notes and Thoughts

By George, I've got it! The fist pounding the open palm of the other hand is a way of emphasizing a point. (From Joe Amendola's book *More Than Words Can Express*, unpublished)

Who's Who in Gastronomy

I was given a copy of this booklet over forty years ago by a dear friend of mine, Dietmar Barnikel, AAC (now deceased), who was an avid student of the culinary arts and a great chef. He personally conducted all the research chronicled here in these next few pages. Though I cannot attest to the historical accuracy of these notes, I can give testimony to the integrity of the chef who wrote them down—he was a man of honor, pride, and great humbleness.

Mr. A

Grateful acknowledgement is made to the *Culinarian*, official publication of the Chef's Association of the Pacific Coast, where this material was first published.

It is the custom to name certain dishes after important and famous persons. This was a practice in use as early as the time of the Roman Empire by the Roman epicurean Apicius in his famous cookbook on Roman cookery, *De Re Coquinaria*.

Mainly it was the chef who created new dishes and named them to honor a certain person or guest; or it was an amateur cook connected with some historical place whose name got associated with a certain style of preparation. Here is an alphabetical listing of those names most mentioned on our classical menus, with biographical information, dates, and some of the special garnitures used to identify each dish.

AGNES SOREL (1410–1450): Mistress of King Carl the VII of France, and one of the finest women of her time. Through her influence on the King she helped the needy and poor. Agnes Sorel is now known as a garniture for chicken or meat: Tartlets filled with chicken mousse, garnished with julienne of sautéed mushrooms, pickled tongue, and truffles. The chicken dish is also served with Sauce Allemande.

ALBUFERA: An inland sea seven miles south of Valencia, Spain. After the conquest of Valencia by Marshal L. G. Suchet, Napoleon made him Duke of Albufera (1812) and to honor this event, Chicken Albufera was created. Dish: Chicken filled with rice, truffles, and goose liver covered with Sauce Albufera (chicken sauce with cayenne and diced pimientos) surrounded by tartlets with a filling of truffles, champignons (mushrooms), chicken gizzards, and pickled tongue.

ALEXANDRA (1844–1925): Queen of Great Britain and Ireland. Born in Copenhagen, Denmark in 1844, married to Albert Edward, Prince of Wales, later crowned King Edward VII in 1902. Her beauty and charm won her immense popularity. To honor her, the dish Sole—or Chicken Alexandra—was created. Dish: Poached filet of sole, covered with Sauce Mornay, glazed, garnished with tips of asparagus. For chicken prepare the same way, except add some truffle essence to the sauce.

ALFONS VII (1886–1941): Last king of Spain (exiled 1931) and a great gourmet. Dish: Rolled, poached filet of sole, set on slices of sautéed aubergines (eggplants) covered with a tomato sauce garnished with diced pimentos. Garniture for meat dishes: Mushroom caps on artichoke bottoms covered with Sauce Madeira.

AUBER (1782–1871): Daniel Francois Esprit, famous French musical composer. Composer of about fifty operas (such as "Fra Diavola," "La muette Portici," etc.), song choruses, and overtures (such as "Amour sacre de la patrie"). Director of Music Conservatoire in Paris, Napoleon III made Auber his imperial conductor (maître de Chapelle) in 1857. Garniture for meat (beef or lamb): Artichoke bottoms filled with chicken mousse covered with Sauce Madeira.

BAGRATION (1765–1812): Peter Iwanowitsch, Russian prince and famous Russian general under Tsar Nicholas I. Famous for his battles against the Finns, Poles, and Turks. Died September 1812 at Borodino, where he received a mortal wound. The great French Chef Antonin Careme was in the service of his widow, where he created several dishes. Dishes: Fish: Filet of sole, filled with a fish filling with crawfish butter, rolled, surrounded with tails of crawfish covered with white wine sauce (mixed with champignon puree), glazed. Soup: Fish cream soup with diced filet of sole, crawfish tails, fish dumplings with crawfish butter. Salad: Diced, cooked chicken, artichoke bottoms, fresh celery, cooked salad macaroni mixed with mayonnaise and tomato puree. Garnished with slices of smoked tongue, truffles, parsley, and cooked eggs.

BALZAC (1799–1850): Honore De, famous French novelist, writer of "Comedie Humaine," a series of novels still known today. Also a well-known gourmet and honored in the culinary arts under the following dishes: Fish: Filet of sole, truffle filling, braised, covered with crawfish sauce, garnished with crawfish tails. Meat: Sautéed filets, chicken dumplings, green olives stuffed with a puree of venison, Sauce Chasseur (Hunters sauce).

BART (1651–1702): Jean, French admiral, first served the Dutch Navy, then changed to the French naval service under Louis XIV. Famous for his battles at sea against England. Honored with the following dish: In the middle of a platter a ragout of scallops, champignons, and crawfish tails, surrounded by folded, poached filet of sole covered with Sauce Normande, garnished with small tartlets filled with scallops and shrimps covered with Mornay sauce; glazed.

BAYARD (1472–1524): Pierre-Seigneur du Terrail, famous French commander, born of a noble family near Pontcharra, served under Carl VIII, Louis XII, and Franz I. Garniture for meat: Croutons filled with a farce consisting of goose liver, champignons, and truffles; covered with Sauce Madeira, artichoke bottoms, and slices of smoked tongue.

BEATRICE (1266–1320): Portinari, a Florentine noblewoman loved by Dante and immortalized in his *Divine Comedy.* Dish: Sautéed filet of beef, garnished with artichoke bottoms, carrots, pommes noisette (small potatoes), and morels; served with demi-glace.

BECHAMEL (around 1600; originally Bechameil): Louis De, Marquis De Nointel, a financier who made his fortune during the French Fronde (after the revolution), was appointed to the post of Lord Steward of the Royal household to Louis XIV. The "invention" of Bechamel sauce is attributed to him, but it had been known for a long time (probably invented by a court chef and dedicated to Bechamel). Dish: Basic white cream sauce and variations, consisting of a roux of flour and butter; add white fond, spice, leeks, mushrooms, onions, pepper, salt, and nutmeg; cook, strain, and add cream.

BERCHOUX (1765–1839): Josef, French poet, made a great name for himself in gastronomical literature due to a poem entitled "Le Gastronomie" in 1800, in which he praised the kitchen from the past to the present in his unique verses. The chefs honored him with several dishes. Dishes: Game, pheasant breasts poached in cognac, butter, and lemon juice set in tartlets filled with pheasant mousse; covered with demi-glace mixed with pheasant essence. Sauce: Sauce Allemande with cream and herb butter.

BIGNON (1816–1878): Louis, great restaurateur, last owner of the world-famous Café Riche in Paris. He did not limit his activities only to cookery, but also took a lively interest in vine-growing and agriculture. In 1867 awarded the Legion of Honour, highest French award. Dish: Soft eggs on a ring of chicken farce, covered with a velouté with estragon essence, garnished with estragon leaves and a stripe of demi-glace. Garniture for meat items: Stuffed baked potatoes filled with a sausage filling and butter.

BISMARK (1815–1898): Prince Otto, German statesman and first chancellor of the German Empire. Besides being a political leader, one of his hobbies was good food and drink. Besides the well-known Bismark herring (fresh herring marinated in vinegar, vegetables, and spices), his name is honored under the following dish: Fillet of sole filled with fish farce and truffles, rolled, put on an artichoke bottom, an oyster and mushroom cap on top, covered with a white wine sauce mixed with oyster essence and Hollandaise sauce, glazed, garnished with tartlets filled with a fish ragout of scallops, shrimps, and mushrooms.

BOIELDIEU (1775–1834): Francois-Adrien, French composer of comic operas, such as "Le Calife de Bagdad" (The Caliph of Baghdad) and his greatest masterpiece "La Dame Blanche" (The White Lady). He is honored through the following dishes: Chicken: Chicken breast filled with a mixture of chicken farce, goose liver puree, and truffles, covered with white chicken sauce, garnished with sautéed truffle balls. Soup: Chicken consommé with tapioca, dumplings made of chicken, goose liver and truffles, and diced chicken. Eggs: Diced chicken, goose liver, and truffles bound with Sauce Velouté filled in tartlets, poached eggs; this covered with white chicken sauce.

BOLIVAR (1783–1830): Simon, soldier and statesman, leader of the revolutions that resulted in the independence from Spain of what are now Bolivia (state named after him), Venezuela, Colombia, Peru, Ecuador, and Panama. Dish: Almond biscuit cake with raspberry, sugar glaze.

BOURDALOUE (1632–1704): Louis, French Jesuit and famous preacher. Dishes mostly desserts: Cake: Half-backed shortbread (pastry) with cleaned, precooked apples, covered with Frangipane cream (special vanilla cream with crushed macaroons) and also covered with crushed almond cookies, melted butter, and sugar; glazed in oven. Instead of apples you can use apricots. Banana tartlets: Tartlets half-filled with whipped cream and chestnut cream, then covered with Curacao liquor–marinated banana slices, whipped cream, crushed macaroons, and red cherry.

BRANTOME (1540–1614): Pierre de Bourdeille, French historian and biographer and seigneur, and Abbe de Brantome, City of Brantome (France). Truffles chief article of commerce. Dish: Poached fish with white wine sauce, julienne of vegetables and truffles, bordure of risotto (rice with parmesan cheese).

BRILLAT SAVARIN (1755–1826): Jean Anthelme, French magistrate, politician, and gastronome. Besides his civilian and political careers, he is most famous for his book *La Physiologie Du Gout* (The Physiology of Taste), a gastronomical master work on which he had engaged for a long time, still one of the best of his kind. Several dishes honor him such as:
1) Several Savarin desserts, a cake made with a yeast mixture, soaked in flavored syrup with rum or kirsch (cherry) added, different garnishes.
2) Omelet Brillat Savarin: Omelet filled with meat of woodcock and truffles, woodcock sauce.
3) Game garniture: Tartlets filled with woodcock farce with truffles, Spanish or demi-glace sauce with woodcock essence.

BRISSE (1832–1876): Baron, master of the wolf hunt and author of culinary works. Baton Brisse adopted a picturesque style in his culinary works (similar to Dumas and Brillat Savarin); some recipes were romanticized and in-executable. Culinary works include *Les 366 Menus, La Cuisine en Carême,* and *La Petite Cuisine de Baron Brisse,* etc. Dish: Tournedos with sautéed tomatoes, pommes soufflé (souffleéd potatoes), artichoke bottoms filled with truffle balls, demi-glace sauce.

BYRON (1788–1824): George Noel Gordon, sixth baron, famous English poet known for his works such as: "Childe Harold," "don Juan," and "Manfred Caine." Dish: Sautéed lamb chops, covered with onion puree, baked; sautéed Mouton kidney with cognac and Bryon potatoes. Byron Potatoes: Large baking potatoes, peeled, diced, lightly sautéed in butter; put in casserole, cover with cream and parmesan cheese, over baked.

CHAMBACERES (1753–1824): Jean Jaques Regis De, Duke of Parma, French statesman, arch-chancellor of the first French Empire. He was a celebrated gourmet, and his dinners were utilized by Napoleon as a useful adjunct to the arts of state craft. He is honored with several dishes created by his chef garde manger, such as: Soup Chambaceres: A one-half crayfish and one-half pigeon cream soup with garnitures of pigeon dumplings and stuffed crayfish tails. Soufflé Chambaceres: Almond soufflé with chopped Angelica, served with a filbert nut cream sauce.

CAMBRIDGE (1774–1850): Adolphus Frederick, youngest son of King George III of England, English general, vice-king of Hanover. Was one of the first English dukes who had in his service a French chef. From him we have the following sauce: Sauce Cambridge (cold): Finely ground capers, cooked egg yolks, and anchovies; whip it with oil (like mayonnaise), add mustard, vinegar, cayenne pepper, and chopped herbs such as dill, parsley, tarragon.

CANOVA (1757–1822): Antonio, Marquis of Ishis, famous Italian sculptor, born in a family of stonemasons, rich family helped him to study under Bernardo. It is said that the boy's genius was discovered through a lion he had modeled in butter. He studied and worked all over Europe. Some of his famous works are: "Amor and Psyche" (Louvre, Paris), "Perseus with the Head of Medusa" (Vatican), "Napoleon I" (Milan), "Venus" (Rome), and "The Three Graces" (Hermitage Gallery, Leningrad). He is honored with the following: Garniture for Tournedos: Sauté filets, slice goose liver, cover with Sauce Madeira, surround with artichoke bottoms filled with a ragout of chicken and chicken livers, kidneys, and truffles with Sauce Madeira.

CAREME (1784–1833): Antoine, famous French chef, genius in his profession, born into a large, poor family; his father sent him on his way after a farewell "dinner" in a tavern when he was only twelve. He started in a simple cook shop, worked himself up through several masters in his profession to the king's household. Later he became the chef of the kings all over Europe. Famous also for his elaborate creations of cakes. Published several books in culinary arts. Some of his dishes and garnitures are: Fish garniture: Poached, cream sauce, fish dumplings, slices of truffles, pastry half moons. Garniture for meat: Olives filled with ham mousse, potato croquettes, and Sauce Madeira. Filet of Sole Carême: No. 2 poached sole, trout milk, cooked oysters, and mushroom caps, covered with white wine sauce with puree of celery roots.

CARNOT (1837–1894): Marie François Sadi, Fourth President of the Third French Republic. Honored with the following dishes: Dessert: Ice Bombe: Outer layer with raspberry ice cream filled with maraschino ice cream, garnished with vanilla whipped cream, cherries, and macaroons. Garniture for meat: Cooked cucumber filled with veal stuffing, red wine sauce with tarragon leaves.

CASANOVA (1725–1798): Giovanni Jacupo, probably Chevalier de Seingalk, Italian adventurer, know through his amorous memoirs, last librarian of Earl Waldstein. Casanova Sauce: Mayonnaise with diced, cooked egg yolks and julienne of cooked egg white and truffles. Fish garniture: Cooked fish with oysters, scallops, and truffles in white wine sauce.

CAVOUR (1810–1861): Count Camillo Benso di, Italian statesman, premier of Italy from 1852–1861, helped unify the Italian kingdom. Honored with the following dishes: Stuffed chicken including truffles, then poached, served with chicken cream sauce and egg noodles. Garniture for meat: Sauté champignons with chestnut puree in tartlets.

CHAMBORD (1820–1883): Henri, Charles Ferdinand Marie Dieudonne, Comte de, the "King Henry V" of the French legitimists. Dish: Carp (fish) stuffed with fish farce, champignons, and truffles closed, poached in red wine, glazed. Garniture for fish: Fish dumplings with truffles, mushroom caps, cooked crayfish, toast points. Sauce Chambord (fish sauce): Sauté rest of fish, fish bones, carrots, onions, celery, parsley, mushrooms, bay leaves, thyme, pepper, flour, red wine and fish stock, strain mix with Spanish fish sauce, Madeira, and anchovy butter.

CHARLES X (1757–1836): King of France from 1824–1830, brother of Ludwig XVIII, gourmet. Chef Eduardo Nignon honored him in a recipe that he got from his master chef, who was in the service of the king. Dish: Roast Rack of Veal: Clean from the veal filet, goose liver, lard, make farce including truffles, fill roast and braise this with Malvasier wine, garnish with tartlets filled with kidney ragout, braised celery roots, and timbales of artichoke puree.

CATRES (1840–1901): Robert, Duke of Catres, son of Ludwig Philippe I, King of France. Served in the French Army during the 1870/71 German-French War under a false name because it was forbidden for a former nobleman to come back to France. (Chartres also a city of northwestern

France, famous for its cathedral, which is a landmark on the plain of Beauce, town is famous for its game-pies generally à la Chartres means with estragon). Fish: Poach fish in white wine with fish stock and estragon, make cream sauce, cover fish, garnish with estragon leaves. Meat: Demi-glace with estragon essence, garnish with estragon leaves.

CHATHAM (1708–1778): William Pitt, first earl of Chatham, English statesman (also a city in Kent, England). In the *Gastronomie* he is honored under the following dish: Larded veal roast, braised, surrounded with slices of pickled tongue, onion sauce with sliced champignons, buttered egg noodles.

CHATEAUBRIAND (1768–1848): François-Rene, Viscomte de, famous French author and politician. Went through different schools and colleges, joined the Knights of Malta. In 1791 he departed for America to take part in a romantic scheme for the discovery of the northwest passage, returned after seven-month stay in America with new ideas, in his work "Natchez" he portrayed the life of the red Indians. Other famous works are "Le-génie du Christianisme," "Atala," and "Mémoires d'outre—tombe." Honored by a double filet from the center, grilled, served with chateau potatoes, assorted vegetables, serve with Sauce Béarnaise or Sauce Colbert.

CHESTERFIELD (1694–1773): Phillip Dormer Stanhope, Earl of Chester field, English statesman and writer, vice-king of Ireland, secretary of state, famous for his literary work, "Letter to His Son," in which he wrote about education, wisdom, and manners in society. (Chesterfield also a market town in Derbyshire, England.) Garniture for fish dishes: Slices of lobster with Sauce Genoise (brown sauce with red wine, fish stock, anchovies, butter, mushrooms, chopped parsley) and diced truffles.

CHEVREUSE (1600–1679): Marie de Rohan-Montbacon, French duchess. Had an important part during the French Fronde (Louis XIV). À la Chevreuse is always served with semolina (cream of wheat) in any form. Tournedos Chevreuse: Filet sautéed, set on round-backed semolina croquettes (mixed with mushrooms), sliced truffles, covered with Sauce Bordelaise made with white wine. Fish: Sautéed fish dipped in egg white and truffles, white wine sauce, semolina croquettes.

CHOISEUIL (1719–1785): Étienne-François, Duc de Choiseuil, French statesman, favored by Madame Pompadour and then appointed Ambassador to Rome. (Choiseuil also one of the islands of the Solomon Island on the South Pacific.) Garniture for meat: Artichoke bottoms filled with goose liver mousse and brown champignon sauce.

COLBERT (1619–1683): Jean Baptiste, great French statesman and financier, founder of the Academy of Sciences. Honored with the following dishes: Sauce Colbert: Demi-glacé whipped with butter, chopped parsley, and lemon juice. Consommé Colbert: Beef consommé, vegetable in julienne, eggs. Fish: Filet of sole meuniere filled with maître d' hôtel butter.

COLIGNY (1519–1572): Gaspard De, French admiral, leader of the Protestants, died for their cause in the Bartholomaeus night. Dish: Sauté tournedos, put on Duchesse potatoes (made from sweet potatoes), cover with Sauce Provençale.

COLUMBUS (1446–1506): Christopher, Italian seaman and explorer from Genoa, later in the service of Spain, discoverer of America (also several cities in the United States are named after him). Dish: chicken consommé with garniture of tapioca, chicken dumplings and diced tomatoes, diced egg royal.

CONDE (1612–1686): Louis II, de Bourbon, Prince de, Duc d' Enghien, called "The Great Conde" because of the many battles he won, a brilliant French general and gourmet. Filet of Sole Conde: Sole poached in mushroom fond, covered with white wine sauce, garnished with strips of tomato puree, glazed. Meat: Any meat garnished with green beans cooked with bacon, brown red wine sauce with diced bacon, whipped with butter. Dessert: Rice pudding ring, in the middle apricots, apricots syrup; bind with cornstarch, add Kirshwasser liquor, garnish with red cherries and mint leaves.

CONTI (1664–1709): Prince François Louis de Bourbon, younger branch of the House of Conde, was chosen as King of Poland, but rivalry took it away. Dish: Braised beef with brown sauce and lentil puree with smoked bacon.

CUMBERLAND (1825–1923): Ernst—August, Duke of Cumberland, also Duke of Brunswick, Lunenburg, by marriage of Princess Thyra of Denmark, later abdicated in 1919. (Cumberland also a county in northwestern England.) The following sauce is the invention of Lord Chanberlain of Malortie who was in the service of the duke. Cumberland Sauce: Currant jelly with port wine, orange juice, with mustard, ginger, cayenne pepper, diced shallots, julienne of orange and lemon peel.

CISSY: Marquis de, Palace Prelate of Napoleon I, one of the finest gastronome of his time, wrote "Gastronomie Historique." Dishes: Pheasant consommé: With cognac and Madeira, julienne of truffles and pheasant dumplings with chestnut. Chicken Cussy: Braised chicken with truffles in Sauce Madeira, mushroom caps filled with artichoke puree, covered with Sauce Madeira.

DEMIDOFF (1813–1870): Anatole, Russian prince, came from a noble Russian family. Made his wealth in mining. Famous scientist and most celebrated gastronome of the second empire. Honored mostly through Chicken Demidoff: Braised chicken casserole with sliced carrots, turnips, onions, and celery and truffles and chicken fond. Fish Demidoff: Boiled fish in demi-glace sauce with truffles, shrimp meat, olives, champignons, and fish dumplings.

DEJEZET (1798–1875): Pauline Virginia, French actress. In 1820 she started to play soubrette and "breeches" parts at the Gymnase with such success that such parts became known as "Dejazets." A French chef honored her with the following: Fish Dejazet: Fish, breaded, sautéed, served on half-melted estragon butter, garnished with lemon and estragon leaves.

DERBY (1865–1948): Edward George Villiers Stanley, seventeenth Earl of Derby, English statesman, minister of war from 1916–1918. He introduced the draft law, ambassador in Paris 1918–1920. Escoffier created for him the Poularde Derby: Chicken filled with a mixture of rice, diced goose liver, truffles with demi-glace, sautéed chicken; when finished garnish with champagne-marinated truffles and demi-glacé with truffle fond.

DESCARTES (1596–1650): René, greatest French philosopher and mathematician. His astonishing analytical genius was displayed in the invention of coordinate geometry and his contributions to theoretical physics, methodology, and metaphysics. Honored with the following: Artichoke Bottoms Descartes: Bottoms filled with a farce of goose liver, veal, truffles, and white Bordeaux wine. Chicken or Quails Descartes: Tartlets of puff filled with a ragout of chicken (or quails) mixed with truffles.

DORIA: Ancient Genoesa family (Italy), the most famous of this family was Andrea Doria (1468–1560), sea admiral and statesman. Charles V made him Imperial Admiral and Prince of Melfi for his successful battles at sea against the pirates and Turks. All dishes â la Doria are with cucumber in any form, sautéed in butter; for fish dishes add diced lemon and lemon juice and brown butter.

D'ORSAY (1801–1825): Count Alfred Giullaume Gabriel, famous dandy and wit, son of General D'Orsay. Garniture: Chateau potatoes, stuffed olives, champignons, and Sauce Madeira.

DUBARRY (1746–1793): Comtesse Marie Jeanne Bécu, French adventuress, mistress of Louis XV, died later under the guillotine. Dubarry Soup: Cauliflower cream soup à la Dubarry is any dish with cauliflower as main garniture.

DUBOIS (1826–1881): Urbain, chef of German Emperor Wilhelm I, writer of gastronomical books such as *La Cuisine Classique* and *La Cuisine Artistique*. Chicken or Quails à la Dubois: Sauté chicken (or quails) with white wine and demi-glacé, serve on a duxelles farce, covered with above sauce; garniture is champignons and chicken dumplings.

DUGLERE: Chef at the famous Café Anglais in Paris, France. Especially known for his Filet of Sole à la Dugler: Sole poached in white wine with chopped shallots, tomatoes, fine herbs, serve with the reduced fond, and as mentioned in the introduction.

DUMAS (1802–1870): Alexandre, French novelist and dramatist, famous gourmet, son of General Dumas, born in San Domingo (Caribbean). Filet of Sole Dumas: Poached with white wine and fines herbs, covered with white fish sauce, garnished with peeled and diced tomatoes. Calf Sweetbread Dumas: Cooked sweetbread, sautéed with artichoke bottoms (diced) and chicken cream sauce. Dumas Sauce (cold): Vinegar, oil, Worchester sauce, chopped shallots and chives (served with oysters).

DUROC (1772–1813): Duc De Friuli, French general and marshall to Napoleon I. Honored here—probably by Chef Carême—with Poularde Duroc: Chicken stuffed with a farce of chicken liver, truffles, and calf's tongue, sautéed, served with truffle slices and Sauce Madeira.

DUSE (1859–1924): Eleanor, world famous Italian actress, born into a family of actors near Venice, she died during a tour in Pittsburg, Pennsylvannia. Filet of Sole à la Duse: Stuffed sole with fish farce, poached, set on pilaf rice; cover with cheese sauce, gratinée, garnish with shrimp and truffles.

DUXELLES: Derives from Uxel and will follow under letter U.

EDWARD VII (1498–1558): Albert, son of Queen Victoria, King of Great Britain and Ireland (1901–1910), also a Bon Vivant and gastronome. Escoffier honored him with the Poularde Edward VII: Chicken stuffed with risotto, truffles, and goose liver; cook, cover with chicken cream sauce with a touch of curry and diced red paprika, garnish with cucumber balls in cream sauce.

ELEONORE (1498–1558): Of Austria, sister of Emperor Charles V, Queen of Portugal, then wife of Franz I of France. Filet of Sole Eleanore: Poach sole, serve on sautéed sliced lettuce, cover with fish velouté and paprika.

ELISABETH (1207–1231): Saint, daughter of Andrew II, King of Hungary, wife of Louis IV, then landgrave of Thuringia (Germany), known for her charity to the poor. Was canonized by Gregory IX in 1235. In memory to her the Omelet en Surprise à la Elisabeth was created: Vanilla ice cream with violets, covered with meringue, garnished with cooked and pulled sugar and violets of sugar.

ESCOFFIER (1847–1935): Auguste, born in Villeneuve-Loubet, France, the most famous French chef, called the "King of Chefs and the Chef of Kings," he pursued his culinary art mostly in England. He was the chef in the Savoy and later in the Carlton Hotel in London, where he retired in 1921 at the age of seventy-four. He practiced his art for sixty-two years. He created many dishes (as mentioned in this series) that are also incorporated in his culinary writings such as *Le Guide Culinaire*, *Le Livre de Menus*, *Ma Cuisine*, and *Le Carnet D'Epicure*.

ESTERHAZY (1765–1833): Prince Miklos (Nicholas) of noble Magyar family (Hungarian-Austrian Monarchy), general, famous for his collections of paintings and engravings. Honored with Goulas Esterhazy: Diced beef, braised with sliced onions, garlic, paprika, thyme, bay leaves, later mixed with julienne of celery roots, parsley roots, and carrots; just before serving add sour cream.

FAVART (1710–1792): Charles Simon, French dramatist, born in Paris, son of a pastry chef. Garniture for meat: Egg noodles with butter and julienne of truffles.

FLAMICHE (1654–1743): Legrand Aussy, a French scholar. Flamiche is a leek tart. Pie pan is lined with pastry dough, filled with sautéed leeks, mixed with egg yolks and butter, spiced; cover with thin layer of pastry, bake in hot oven, serve at once. Eaten mostly in the Burgundy and Picardy regions of France. In some parts of France it is also made with rum or brandy or sugar filling.

FLEURY (1654–1743): Andre Hercule de, French cardinal, later First Minister to Louis XV. Garniture for meat: Potato croquette rounds filled with a ragout of veal kidneys mixed with demi-glacé and tomato paste.

FRANCATELLI (1850–1901): Charles Elmé, chef of Swiss decent of Queen Victoria of England, also author of *The Cook's Guide,* he created several dishes. One of these is Risolles Francatelli, thin pancakes (crêpes) filled with pheasant puree, chilled, cut, breaded, sautéed in butter, served with a pepper sauce and currant jelly.

FRANCOIS I (1494–1547): King of France and one of the biggest eaters of his time. Honored with the following: Tartlets filled with poached eggs, covered with a ragout of carp (fish) and truffle in white wine sauce.

FRANKLIN (1706–1790): Benjamin, American philosopher, statesman, and man of letters. Fish: Cooked, Sauce Normande with truffles, champignons, shrimp and sliced lobsters, fish dumplings. Meat: Stuffed, braised whole onions, pan-fried potatoes.

FRANZ JOSEPH I (1830–1916): Emperor of Austria, King of Hungary, honored in the culinary arts with a Vanilla Soufflé: Maraschino liquor–marinated fruits, covered with a chocolate sauce and whipped cream with Kirsch liquor.

FRASCATI: A hillside town, near Rome (Italy), formerly a stronghold of the Counts of Tusculum, now many fine villas of the Roman nobility. Garniture for meat: Sautéed slices of goose liver, asparagus tips, small mushrooms, truffle balls, and potato croquettes with diced truffles, demi-glacé sauce with port.

GAMBETTA (1838–1882): Leon, French statesman. Garniture for meat: Small stuffed eggplants with baked tomatoes.

GAVARNI (1804–1866): Pseudonym of Hippolyte Sulpice Guillaume Chevalier, French caricaturist. In 1833 in the journal *des Gens du Monde* he began a series of lithographed sketches, in which he portrayed the striking characteristics, the foibles, and the vices of the various classes of French society. Honored with Trout Gavarni: Lightly sauté trout, fill with maître d' hôtel butter, roll in aluminum foil and bake in oven till done, serve with boiled potatoes in nut butter. Turbot Gavarni: Poached; serve with Hollandaise sauce with diced truffles.

GLOUCESTER (1776–1834): William Frederick, Duke of Gloucester, British marshall (Gloucester also city and county in England, also two cities in United States). Title of the Dukes of Gloucester mostly the younger princes of the English kings. Gloucester sauce: Thick mayonnaise mixed with sour cream, lemon juice, Worcestershire sauce, mustard, cayenne pepper, and fennel.

GODARD (1849–1895): Benjamin Louis Paul, French composer. Chiefly remembered for the "Berceuse" from his opera "Jocelyn." Honored in the culinary arts with the following dishes: Meat: Veal quenelles (dumplings) mixed with truffles and champignons, cock's combs and kidneys, mushroom caps, brown Godard sauce. Poultry: Braised chicken, same garnish as above-mentioned except chicken quenelles, white Godard sauce. Godard Sauce (brown): Demi-glacé cooked with mirepoix, ham, white wine, and champignon fond, strained; at last minute whip soft butter under it. Godard Sauce (white): White wine sauce with champignon fond, diced ham, and mushrooms.

GOUFFE (1807–1877): Jules, former chef of the exclusive Jockey Club in Paris, writer of several books on culinary arts. Meat garniture: Forms of risotto rice, veal quenelles, champignons, and truffles in olive form, Madeira sauce. Another garnish is little nests of Duchesse potatoes fried and hollowed out to hold chanterelles cooked in cream sauce, asparagus tips in butter.

GOUNOD (1818–1893): Charles François, French composer, born in Paris, famous for his composition of Shakespeare's "Romeo and Juliet." Honored with Chicken Gounod: Sauté chicken, flambé with cognac, add champignon and truffles, artichokes and carrots, demi-glace with tomatoes.

GRAMONT (1819–1888): Antoine, Agenor Alfred, Duc de Gramont, Duc de Guiche, Prince de Bidache. French diplomat and statesman, minister of foreign affairs. Nignon (famous chef of the restaurant Larue in Paris) created for him Pheasant Gramont: Pheasant stuffed with a farce of veal sausage, goose liver, truffles, and chestnut puree, roasted flamed with cognac, pheasant jus, served with celery hearts and beef marrows.

GRIMALDI (1606–1680): Giovanni Francesco, Italian architect, painter, and engraver, from Genoese nobility. Garniture for fish: Ragout with small macaroni, diced champignons, truffles, and scampi in cream sauce, mixed with lobster butter.

HALEVY (1834–1908): Ludovic, French author, born in Paris, wrote in every branch of literature, member of the Conservatoire, Comedie Française, and Society of Dramatic Authors. Honored with Fish Halevy: Fish cooked, covered with Sauce Montreuil, sprinkled on top with diced truffles and lobster (if possible lobster eggs).

HATZFELD (1848–1910): Herman, German Prince of Hatzfeld, also Duke of Trachenberg, first cup bearer for the Prussian king. Honored with Consommé Hatzfeld: Pheasant consommé garnished with julienne of celery roots and pheasant breasts, sherry wine.

HELOISE (1101–1164): Niece of Kanoniker Fulbert, famous for her unsuccessful love of the Monk Abelard. Fish Heloise: Poach fish on a bed of sliced mushrooms and diced shallots with white wine; reduce fond, bind, add a touch of Glace de Viande and whip up with butter and lemon juice, cover fish.

HENRY IV (1553–1610): King of France, son of Antoine de Bourbon, Duke of Vendome. He was the king who promised all his people a chicken in every pot on Sunday, that means he tried to restore prosperity to his kingdom. Garniture for meat or chicken: Potato balls sautéed in butter, glazed with glace de viande filled in artichoke bottoms, Sauce Béarnaise on the side.

HOHENLOHE (1819–1901): Schillingfuerst Chlodwig Karl, comes from a German princely family which took its name from the district of Hohenlohe in Franconita. Prince of Hohenlohe, German chancellor (1894–1900), was a great statesman under Bismarck. Honored with a garniture for meat: Sauté goose liver, mignon potatoes, and artichoke bottoms filled with estragon puree covered with Sauce Choron.

HOLSTEIN (1837–1909): Fredrick of Holstein, counselor in the political department of the German Foreign Office (1878–1906), was the most important personality, after Bismarck, in the wine restaurant of F. W. Borchardt, Berlin, where he used to dine. The chef created for him Veal Cutlet Holstein: Breaded veal cutlet, sautéed, fried egg on top; sprinkle with capers, surround with toasted canapés of smoked salmon, anchovies, and sardines; pickles, beets, and pan-fried potatoes served on the side.

HUNYADI (1387–1456): John, Hungarian statesman and brilliant warrior. He defeated the Turks in Amselfeld (1448) and shortly before his death, he successfully defended Belgrade against Mohammed II. The thankful Hungarians honored him in the culinary arts with Goulash Hunyadi: Pork goulash with sour cream, a bit of diced pickles, and diced potatoes.

ISABELLE DE FRANCE (1225–1270): Daughter of Philippe IV of France, wife of King Edward II of England. Remembered with the following dish:

Poulet Isabelle: Fill chicken with risotto rice, mixed with scampi tails and truffles, poached in half Chablis wine and half white fond; after it is cooked make chicken cream sauce from the fond; garnish with champagne-cooked truffles.

ISMAILA (1830–1895): Khedive of Egypt, was born in Cairo, being the second of the three sons of Abraham, and grandson of Mohammed Ali. Dish: Poached fish with herbs, champignons served on pilaf rice mixed with green peas and red pimientos; reduce fond of fish; whip it up with butter and cover fish.

JACKSON (1767–1845): Andrew, U.S. soldier, statesman, and seventh president of the United States. Born in Waxhaw, Lancaster County, South Carolina, his parents immigrated from Ireland. Dishes: Cream Soup Jackson: Potato cream soup with green beans, julienne of leek and tapioca. Fish Jackson: Cooked fish with small white onions, covered with fish cream sauce, chopped parsley, garnished with baked half-moons of puff pastry.

JANIN (1804–1874): Jules Gabriel, French critic and writer, famous gastronome. Filet of Sole Janin: In white-wine-poached sole, put on Duxelles, garnish with scampi tails, scallops, and truffles, cover with reduced fond mixed with turtle sauce and scampi butter.

JOINVILLE (1818–1900): François Ferdinand Philippe Louis Marie, Prince de Joinville, third son of Louis Phillippe, Duc D' Orleans, King of France. Dishes: Fish Joinville: Poached sole covered with a ragout of crabs, truffles, and mushrooms, garnished with truffle slices and scampi tails covered with Sauce Joinville. Sauce Joinville: Fish velouté with mushrooms fond, oyster water, diced crab; bind with egg yolk and cream, whip it up with crab butter.

JOSEPHINE (1763–1814): Maire Rose J. Tacher de la Pagerie, Vicomtesse de Beauharnais, Empress of France, first wife of Napoleon I. She favored sweets, and we honor her with the following dish: Pudding Josephine: Cook half-fresh peaches in vanilla sugar with water; when cooled off put a half peach on sweet rice, cover with raspberry sauce, garnish with whipped cream.

JOUFFROY (1796–1842): Theodore Simon, French philosopher. Fish Jouffroy: Fish poached in Pouilly wine (French white wine), sautéed champignons on top; cover with fish cream sauce, glace; garnish with patty shells filled with green asparagus tips topped with a slice of truffle.

JULES VERNE (1828–1905): Famous French writer, mostly novels. Honored with a garniture for meat dishes: Small round roasted potatoes, glazed white turnips; bind with beef jus glace.

JUSSIEU: The name of a French family distinguished for its botanists. Honored in the culinary arts is Adrien Laurient Henri de Jussieu

(1797–1853), born in Paris. His favored dish was Beef Braise: Sautéed brussels sprouts, small glazed onions, and the fond of the braised beef mixed with Sauce Madeira.

KLEBER (1753–1800): Jean-Baptiste, French general, son of a builder, trained as architect, nominated to a military school in Munich, successful general under Napoleon. Killed by a fanatic in Cairo. Tournedos à la Kleber: Fillet of beef sauté on toast, truffle sauce; as garniture artichoke bottom with goose liver.

KLEOPATRA (51–30 BC): Cleopatra, Queen of Egypt, known for her beauty and political intrigues, spoke several Mideast languages. Fish Kleopatra: Filet of sole filled with a white fish farce with truffles, poached with white wine and champignon fond, covered with white wine sauce and slices of truffles.

LADY MORGAN: An English writer. In one of her travels to France she was invited to dinner by Baron Rothschild where she met Antoine Carême who then created for her Chicken Cream Soup Lady Morgan: With garniture of rice, diced chicken, and cock's comb. Meat garniture: Diced cock's comb, corn, and mallow in Madeira sauce with pan-fried potatoes.

LAFAYETTE (1757–1834): French politician and general. This freedom fighter is honored with a garniture for fish: Poached sole covered with white wine sauce and tomato concassé, sprinkled on top with julienne of truffles, surrounded with prawns or shrimp.

LAGUIPIERE: Chef of Napoleon I, then Murat, Carême's tutor in all branches of cookery. He accompanied Murat to Naples, then to Russia, where he froze to death at the river Beresina near Vilno during the retreat in 1812 from Moscow. Creator of many dishes, but only a few bear his name. Crêpes Laguipiere: French pancakes filled with chocolate butter mixed with roasted, chipped nuts flamed with cognac and Cointreau. Consommé Laguipiere: Pheasant consommé with eggs royale, pheasant dumplings, poached pigeon egg, and sherry wine. Fish Laguipiere: Poached fish, white wine sauce with sliced mushrooms, scallops, and fish dumplings.

LAMBALLE (1749–1792): Marie Therese Louise of Savoy-Carignano, Princesse de Lamballe. Born in Turin, Italy married to Prince de Lamballe of Penthievre of France. Dish: Tapioca soup with diced chicken and green peas, red pimientos.

LA PEROUSE (1741–1788): Jean François de Galaup, Comte De La Perouse, French navigator, discoverer of the North-West passage, navigator and explorer of the Pacific, where he lost his life battling the sea. Dish: Fish filled, poached covered with sliced lobster, topped with Sauce Genoese with crabmeat, shrimp and fish dumplings, lobster eggs.

LAVALIERE (1644–1710): Duchess Louise Francoise de la Baum de Blanc, mistress of Louis XIV of France. Garniture for meat: Artichoke bottoms filled with asparagus tips, chateau potatoes, Bordeaux sauce.

LENCLOS (1620–1705): Ninon de Lenclos, an interesting and inspiring beauty. Her salon was the center of the social life in Paris. It is said she still was a beauty when she was eighty years old. Honored in the culinary arts with a garniture for Tournedos or Lamb-chops: Sauté meat, set on Mireille potatoes, cover with Madeira sauce whipped with butter, garnish with pastry shells filled with asparagus tips and truffles.

LEO X (1475–1521): Jean of Medici, pope from 1513–1521, called "the Magnificent," a connoisseur of art and literature, including the culinary arts. It is recorded that he was the first to serve Veal Fricandeau in his house.

LESZCYNSKI (1677–1766): Stanislaus, King of Poland, Duke of Lothringen, father-in-law of Louis XV of France, famous gastronome who served for the first time in his house the Babe. Ragout of Turkey Wings Leszcynski: Turkey wings filled with farce, braised, served with a brown champignon sauce with truffles, sweetbread, and pickles.

LONDONBERRY (1778–1854): Charles William Stewart Vane, third Marquis of Londonberry, British general, diplomat. His chef created for him the following dish: Veal Cream Soup: Bind with egg yolk and cream, some Madeira wine and turtle meat (diced).

LOUIS XIV (1638–1715): King of France known as "The Great," died September 1, 1715, after the longest reign in European history at this time. Tournedos Louis XIV: Sauté tournedos set on Anna potatoes, artichoke bottoms filled with mushroom farce; top with slice of truffle, Devil sauce.

LOUIS XV (1710–1774): King of France, he was the grandson of Louis XIV. He was known for his many mistresses such as Madame Pompadour, Madame De Barry, etc., who are also recorded in these series. Also known for his lavish feasts and the advancement of the French culinary arts during his reign. Fish Louis XV: Filet of sole poached in white wine, chipped lobster on top, covered with white wine sauce, surrounded with baked half moons. Garniture for meat: Diced artichoke bottoms, truffles, mushrooms, brown truffle sauce.

LOUVOIS (1641–1691): François Michel de Teller, Marquis de Louvois, French statesman and war minister to King Louis XIV. Honored with the dish Peach Louvois: In a glass bowl, a round of cake (biskuitboden), raspberry jelly, sweet rice pudding, fresh peaches poached in orange syrup, decorated with cherry mint leave and ring of whipped cream or squares of Blancmange pudding.

LUCULLUS (114–57 BC): Lucius Licinius, surnamed Ponticus, Roman general. He was very rich; after unsuccessful mingling in politics, he retired into that elegant leisure, that luxury refined by good taste and tempered philosophy, for which he has become proverbial, one of the famous gourmets of his time. Poularde Lucullus: Chicken filled with chicken farce and truffles, sautéed, covered with truffle sauce and with champagne-cooked truffles; cock's comb garnished. Meat garniture: Truffles cooked in Madeira then filled with chicken kidney farce; chicken dumplings with truffles, diced cock's comb and demi-glacé sauce.

LULLY (1633–1687): Jean Baptiste, musician, French composer, of Italian birth, first scullery boy for Madame de Montpensier. For his musical talents sent to music school, became director of Court Orchestra, founder and first director of Opera of Paris, introduced the Menuette to the court. Egg Lully: Fried egg set on macaroni mixed with tomatoes concassé, surrounded with slices of ham. Poularde Lully: Chicken filled with chicken farce, sautéed, covered with chicken cream sauce and garnished with truffles, champignons, and cock's comb.

MAC DONALD (1765–1840): Etienne Jacques, Duke of Tarent, French marshall. Dish: Chicken cream soup with a puree of calf sweetbread, sherry wine, and small diced pickles.

MAC MAHON (1808–1893): Count Marie Edme Patrice Maurice, Duke of Magenta, marshall, a short term as president of the French Republic. Garniture for meat: Chateau potatoes, large bean seeds sautéed in butter, Sauce Madeira with truffles.

MAECENAS (73–8 BC): Gaius Cilnius, Roman patron of letters, his great wealth was in part hereditary, but he owed his position and influence to his connection with Emperor Augustus. He stimulated and helped Haraz, Virgil, and other famous writers. Now honored with Cream Soup Maecenas: A mixture of lobster and chicken cream soup with a garniture of diced lobster, chicken, and truffles.

MAINTENON (1635–1719): Françoise D'Aubigne, Marquise de Maintenon, second wife of Louis XIV. She had a tremendous influence on the King's political affairs. Garniture for meat: Sautéed mushrooms mixed with cream sauce and onion puree, put on sautéed meat, covered with truffle sauce.

MALMESBURY (1746–1820): James Harris, Earl of Malmesbury, English diplomatist. Honored with Ice Punch: Peach sherbet with orange juice and nut liquor, topped with Italian meringue.

MARENGO: A village in northern Italy where Napoleon Bonaparte won his great victory over the Austrians on June 14, 1800. Bonaparte, who on the day of the battle ate nothing until the battle was over, asked his personal Chef Dunand to prepare dinner. But because they were far away from any supply wagons, they had to get what they could find, and this was some eggs, tomatoes, chicken, garlic, oil, crayfish, and a saucepan.

With this Master Chef Dunand prepared Chicken à la Marengo: He sautéed the chicken, added the tomatoes and garlic, flambéed with brandy from the general's flask, and garnished it with fried eggs and crayfish. Bonaparte was so pleased that he gave an order to Chef Dunand to prepare it after every battle.

MARGOT (1553–1615): Queen of Navarre, daughter of Henri II by Catherine de Medici, wife of King Henri IV of Navarre. Famous for her beauty, her learning spirit, and her loose conduct. After the dissolution of her marriage, she still kept the Queen's title, also the King continued to consult her on important political affairs. Famous also for her letters and memoirs, which rank among the best of the sixteenth century. Honored with: Chicken Cream Soup: With almond milk, garnished with chicken dumplings and pistachio puree; Chicken: Stuffed with chicken farce and almond puree, poached, covered with chicken cream sauce with almond milk, garnished with chicken dumplings, pistachio, and crab butter balls.

MARIA STUART (1542–1587): Queen of Scotland. Because she murdered her husband, she was imprisoned for nineteen years then executed by order of Queen Elisabeth I of England. Meat garniture: Tartlets filled with a puree of white turnips and onions, a slice of cooked beef marrow; covered with demi-glace sauce.

MARIA THERESA (1717–1780): Archduchess of Austria, later Queen of Austria, Hungary, and Bohemis, wife of Emperor Francois I. She preferred beef and Viennese pasta dishes. Garniture for meat: Rice croquettes with truffles and demi-glace sauce with tomato puree.

MARIE ANTOINETTE (1755–1793): Queen of France, ninth daughter of Maria Theresa and Emperor Francis I, wife of Louis XIV of France. She was beheaded in 1793 during the French Revolution. Consommé Marie Antoinette: Game consommé with truffles, game dumplings, and gold leaves. Cream Soup Marie Antoinette: Pheasant cream soup with white Bordeaux wine and pheasant dumplings with truffles.

MARIE LOUISE (1791–1847): Queen of France, daughter of Emperor Francis I, was second wife of Napoleon I. Garniture for tournedos and lamb: Artichoke bottoms filled with mushroom and onions, veal jus.

MARIVAUX (1688–1763): Pierre Carlet de Chamberlainde, French novelist and dramatist. The dialogues of his writings gave a new word to the French language: "marivaudage." Filet of sole Marivaux: Poached sole put on rice pilaf, covered with white wine sauce, surrounded with Bercy sauce and tomatoes.

MASCAGNI (1863–1945): Pietro, Italian operatic composer, famous for his one-act opera "Cavalleria Rusticana." Garniture for meat: Tartlets filled with chestnut puree, slice of calf sweetbread, tomato sauce, and straw potatoes.

MASSENA (1756–1817): André, Duke of Rivoli, Prince of Essling, greatest of Napoleon Bonaparte's French marshalls, son of a small wine merchant. Garniture for Tournedos: Artichoke bottoms filled with Béarnaise sauce, on the meat a slice of beef marrow, tomato sauce. Fish: cooked lobster sauce with lobster meat, surrounded with baked oysters.

MASSENET (1842–1912): Jules Emile Frederic, French composer, famous for his operas "Cid" and "Manon." Honored in the culinary arts with Tournedos Massenet: Artichoke bottoms filled with small peas, Anna potatoes; on the meat a slice of beef marrow, Madeira sauce.

MAZARIN (1602–1661): Jules, French cardinal and statesman for Louis XIV of France. Born in Piscina, Italy, later became a naturalized Frenchman. Fish: Poached in white wine, covered with crab sauce, surrounded with tartlets filled with diced shrimp, truffles in shrimp sauce.

MEDICI: The name of a famous noble Italian family dating back to the twelfth century. Honored in the culinary arts was Giacomo Medici (1817–1882), famous Italian soldier. Garniture for meat: Tartlets filled with peas and carrots, potato croquettes filled with sorrel mousse, beef jus. Fish Medici: Sautéed with butter and shallots, diced tomatoes, fried onion rings.

MELBA (1861–1931): Dame Nellie (her real name was Helen Porter Mitchell, *Melba* comes from Melbourne, her favored city). Famous Australian operatic soprano, honored with a dessert. Peach Melba: Fresh peaches poached in vanilla syrup with a few orange peels; put on vanilla ice cream, cover with raspberry sauce, whipped cream, and toasted almonds.

METTERNICH (1773–1859): Prince Winneberg, Clemens Wenzel Lothar, Austrian statesman and diplomatist, for forty years he served the Austrian monarchy. He was a gourmet; in his house they served for the first time chestnut pudding. He is also known for his Rack of Veal Metternich: Braise rack of veal, slice, then put it back on with a Béchamel sauce with paprika, truffle slices; cover with same sauce, sprinkle with cheese and bake.

MEYERBEER (1791–1864): Giacomo, German composer (first known under Jakob Meyer Beer), music director to the King of Russia. Eggs Meyerbeer: Fried eggs with grilled lamb kidneys and truffle sauce.

MICHELANGELO (1475–1564): M. Buonarrati, the most famous of the great Florentine artists of the Renaissance, Italian sculptor, painter, poet, famous for his Sistine Chapel in Rome. The chef, Jules Lefort, of Prince Metternich honored him with Pudding à la Michelango: Soufflé pudding with chestnut flour, cacao powder; surrounded with glazed chestnuts and served with chocolate sauce.

MILTON (1608–1674): John, English poet, famous for his writings *Paradise Lost* and *Paradise Regained*. Chicken Milton: Poached chicken, covered with chicken cream sauce, garnished with cock's comb, chicken kidneys, slices of truffles, and green asparagus spears.

MIRABEAU (1749–1791): Honore Gabriel Riqueti, Comte de, French statesman, president of the French National Assembly, famous gourmet. Garniture for gilled beef: Crosswise slices of anchovies, olives estragon leaves, and anchovy butter.

MONSELET (1825–1888): Charles, French writer and gourmet, famous for his culinary writings "Lettres Gourmandes," "Gastronome," "Cuisine Practique," and others. Tournedos Monselet: Stuffed eggplants, Parisian potato balls, Foyot sauce.

MONTAGNE (1885–1948): Prosper, famous chef. He was chef for Des Pavillons d'Armenonville, Des Pavillons Ledoyen, and The Grand Hotel in Paris. Well known through his culinary writings; one of them is *Grand Larousse Gastronomique*. Every year in Paris there is a "Prosper Montagne Award" where famous chefs compete. Tournedos Montagne: Artichoke bottoms with champignon mousse, filled tomatoes, veal gravy.

MONTAIGNE' (1533–1592): Michel de, Seigneur de, French philosopher and writer, famous for his essays. Dish: Almond biscuit with chopped orange marmalade in brioche form, glazed with apricot marmalade and orange fondant.

MONTESQUIEU (1689–1755): Charles Louis de Secondant, Baron de la Brede et de, French writer and philosophical historian. Honored with Timbale of Goose Liver Montesque: A buttered timbale form sprinkled with cooked, diced eggs, filled with chicken, goose liver farce, and a ragout of truffles and goose liver, poached, turned over, and served with Madeira.

MONTEGELAS (1759–1838): Josef, Prince of Montegelas, son of an old noble family of Savoyards, his father was general to the elector of Bavaria. Dish: Patty shell filled with a ragout of goose liver, mushrooms, sweetbread, beef tongue, truffles, and Madeira sauce.

MONTMIRELL (around 1800–1900): Famous French chef. Was for many years the chef for Chateaubriand and is mentioned in Chateaubriand's memoirs. Timbale Pheasant Montmirell: Timbale laid out with slices of truffles filled with pheasant farce, and a ragout of mushrooms, goose liver, cock's comb with Madeira sauce; garnished with pheasant breasts and pickled tongue.

MONTPENSIER (1814–1890): Prince de Antoine-Marie Philippe Louis d' Orleans, son of King Philippe of France. Garniture for meat: Green asparagus tips, truffle slices, demi-glace with white wine whipped with butter.

MORNAY (1549–1623): Philippe de, Seigneur de Plessis-Marly, French statesman, famous for the dishes covered with a cheese sauce à la Mornay.

MORNY (1811–1865): Charles Auguste Louis Joseph, Duc de, called "Comte de," half-brother of Napoleon III, helped the coup d'etat on December 2, 1851. Honored with Filet of Sole Mornay: Poached, served with Italian sauce, garnished with Anna potatoes.

MURAT (1767–1815): Joachim, King of Naples, brother in law of Napoleon I, marshall. Fish Murat: Filet of sole sautéed in butter, mixed with tomato slices and chopped parsley, covered with a meat glace whipped with butter and lemon juice.

MURILLO (1617–1682): Bartholomew Esteban, Spanish painter, honored with Consommé Murillo: Chicken consommé with small noodles, diced tomatoes, and chervil leaves. Chicken Breasts Murillo: Chicken breasts covered with champignon puree, baked, garnished with fresh tender vegetables, covered with butter whipped up with chicken jus.

NANSEN (1861–1930): Fridjob, Norwegian explorer, artist, statesman, and humanitarian, awarded the 1922 Nobel Peace Prize. Honored with a Cold Salmon a la Nansen: Poached, cold salmon glazed with aspic, with julienne of vegetables in geleé, cold half-stuffed tomato or cucumbers filled with caviar-surrounded mayonnaise.

NAVARIN: The name "Navarin," famous for the French Mouton ragout, is not named after a person but the Greek city of Navarino—today called Pylo—where the famous sea battle of Navarino at 1872 was fought between the English-French-Russian Navy and the Turkish-Egyptian Navy.

NELSON (1758–1805): Horatio, Viscount, Duke of Bronte in Sicily, British naval hero, famous for his many successful sea battles. Meat: 1: Small steaks sautéed on both sides, covered with a farce and onion puree, sprinkled with white bread crumbs, baked in oven, Madeira sauce. 2: Large piece of meat roasted, sliced, then put together with onion puree and slices of bacon, on top some cheese soufflé batter with truffles, baked, Madeira sauce. Fish: On a round platter, in the middle potatoes noisette surrounded with poached fish covered with white wine sauce and scallops, garnished.

NEUMOURS (1814–1895): Louis Charles Philippe Raphael, Duke de Neumours, second son of the Duke of Orleans, afterward King Louis Philippe. Garniture for meat (roast): Vichy carrots, buttered peas, and sautéed Parisian potato balls, meat fond. Fish: Filet of sole, filled with fish farce, poached in white wine; lay it in a circle on a platter, cover with shrimp sauce, garnish with slices of truffles, in the middle fill it with a ragout of champignons, fish dumplings, and Sauce Normande, further garnish with shrimp croquettes with truffles.

NESSELRODE (1780–1862): Karl Robert, Duke de Nesselrode, Russian statesman and famous gourmand. Garniture for meat: Glazed chestnuts, champignons, stuffed olives and truffles, Madeira sauce with julienne of truffles. Fish: Boned fish filet, filled with lobster farce, surrounded with thickly sliced bacon, rolled in dough, baked; separate lobster sauce with oysters. Pudding a la Nesselrode: Fill form with an alternate layer of Bavarian vanilla cream, biscuit cake marinated with maraschino liquor spread with chestnut puree, Malaga grapes, almond and mandarins, cold wine cream with Malaga wine separate.

NIGNON (1863–1934): Eduardo, famous chef, owner of the Restaurant Larue in Paris, writer of several culinary arts books. One of his colleagues honored him with the following Chicken Cream Soup à la Nignon: Chicken cream soup with pistachio puree, chicken dumplings served on the side, and small patty shells with white asparagus tips.

ORLEANS: Famous French noble family (the House of Orleans) that had a leading role in the history of France. Honored with several dishes such as: Garniture for meat: Sauté endives mixed with egg yolks (raw), creamed potatoes, meat fond separate. Garniture for fish: Poached filet of sole, covered with a ragout of champignons, truffles, and shrimp, garnished with larger prawns covered with shrimp sauce.

ORLOV (1827–1885): Prince, entered the diplomatic service, represented Russia as ambassador successively in Brussels (1860–1870), in Paris (1870–1882), and Berlin (1882–1885). As a publicist he stood in the forefront of reform. His French Chef Georges Bouzou honored him with the Timbale de Volaille Prince Orlov: A timbale laid out with thin crêpes filled with chicken farce, diced pickled tongue and farina, poached, served with a chicken cream sauce. Whether the Rack of Veal Orlov was created by Chef Georges Bouzou is not historically proven. Rack of Veal Orlov: Rack of veal braised, cut in slices, then set together with onion puree and slices of truffles, covered with a mixture of Béchamel sauce and onion puree, glazed, then surrounded with asparagus tips and braised celery, veal jus served on the side.

PALMERSTON (1784–1865): Henry John Temple, third viscount, English statesman. Was the dominating personality in English politics for twenty years. Dish: Brown game soup with champignon and sherry wine, diced bread croutons on the side.

PARMENTIER (1737–1813): Antoine-Auguste, French agronomist, helped to make the potato popular in France. All dishes Parmentier are served with diced potatoes sautéed in butter with fresh chopped parsley.

PATTI (1843–1919): Adelina Juana Maria, famous singer, born in Madrid, Spain, later settled in America. Dishes: Chicken consommé with diced artichoke bottoms, julienne of truffles, and tapioca. Dessert: Strawberries Patti: Strawberries marinated in sugar and Kirshwasser liquor, set on chocolate ice cream, garnished with vanilla-flavored whipped cream.

PETER I (1672–1725): Called "The Great," Emperor of Russia, son of the Tsar Alexius Mikhailovich. Honored with a Beef Consommé Peter I: Consommé with julienne of turnips, celery roots, champignons, lettuce, and truffles.

POLIGNAC (1780–1847): Jules de Polignac, prince, son of Count Jules, an ancient French family. Ambassador to the English Court and later foreign minister under Charles X of France. Filet of Sole Polignac: Sole poached in white wine, butter, and fish fond; after fond reduced, add fish velouté, whip with butter, add precooked julienne of mushrooms and truffles and pour over fish. Chicken Polignac: Chicken filled with a mousse of champignons and truffles, cooked covered with chicken cream sauce with julienne of mushrooms and truffles.

POMPADOUR (1721–1764): Jeanne Antoinette Poisson le Norman D'Etoiles, Marquis de, mistress of Louis XV of France. Honored with several dishes, but here I just want to mention a few. Fish: Breaded with melted butter and bread crumbs, sautéed, slice of truffle, a touch of meat glace, garnished with nut potatoes and Béarnaise sauce with tomato paste. Meat: Sautéed filet, covered with truffle sauce, garnished with round potato croquettes and artichoke bottoms filled with lentil puree.

PRALIN or PRALINE (1598–1675): Cesar de Choiseuil, Comte du Plessis-Pralin, Marshall of France. His name is honored in the history of gastronome through the creation of his cook: Almonds roasted with sugar that can be used for desserts or in baking or can be covered with chocolate.

PRINCE HENRY OF PRUSSIA (1862–1929): Brother of Emperor William II. Dish: Breaded veal chops, sautéed, sautéed diced artichoke bottoms.

PROCOPE (1625–1689): François (actually his full name was Francesco Procopio dei Cultelli), a nobleman of Palermo, Italy. Owner of the famous café Procope in Paris. He created several ice cream bombes, such as the following: Line out form with vanilla ice cream and roasted almonds, then fill with a light strawberry mousse, freeze, unmold, garnish with whipped cream, strawberries, and mint leaves.

PUECKLER-MUSKAU (1705–1771): Herman, Prince of Pueckler-Muskau, famous garden architect and gourmet, writer of many cultural and historical travel reports. The pastry chef Schulz of Lausith, Germany created the Prince Pueckler Ice Bombe: Three layers, first vanilla ice cream with broken up macaroons, then strawberry ice cream, then chocolate ice cream with broken macaroons; when frozen unmold and garnish with whipped cream, red maraschino cherries, and mint leaves.

RABELAIS (1495–1553): French author, medical doctor, and Benedictine monk, famous for his book *Gargantua and Pantagruel*. Honored with Filet of Sole Rabelais: Breaded sole, sautéed in butter, served with a Béarnaise sauce with anchovies purr.

RACHEL (1821–1858): Elisabeth Felix, famous French actress. Garniture for meat: Artichoke bottoms filled with beef marrows, parsley, red wine sauce. Filet of Sole Rachel: Filet filled with fish farce, truffles, poached, covered with fish sauce with diced green asparagus and truffles. Consommé Rachel: Chicken consommé with tapioca, julienne of artichoke bottoms, beef marrows.

RADZIWILL (1803–1834): Elisa, came from the noble family of Lithuania, first love of Emperor William I. Garniture for fish: Fish cooked with carp milk, oysters, champignons, truffle slices, shrimp dumplings, and Genfer sauce.

RAFFAEL (1483–1520): Santi, Italian painter and architect, was one of the builders of St. Peter's Cathedral in Rome . . . , creator of altar pictures and madonnas. Garniture for filet and lamb: Artichoke bottoms filled with creamed potatoes and Béarnaise sauce and creamed baby carrots, straw potatoes.

RAKOCZY (1676–1735): Francis II, prince of a noble Magyar (Hungarian) family, leader of the independence movement against the Habsburg. Garniture for braised meat: Sautéed eggplants in paprika sauce.

RECAMIER (1777–1849): Jeanne Francais Julie Adelaide, famous French woman liked because of her beauty and charm, well known in literary and political circles in Paris, wife of banker Jaques Recamier. Dessert: Peach Recamier: Fresh peaches blanched in vanilla syrup, set on nut ice cream, garnished with whipped cream; cold sabayon served separate.

REJANE (1857–1920): Gavriele, French actress. Escoffier created for her Consommé Rejane: Chicken consommé with chervil, a royale with almond and carrot puree.

REMBRANDT (1606–1669): Harmen van Rijn, famous Dutch painter, born in Leyden, famous for his portraits and historical paintings. Dish: Chicken cream soup mixed with a puree of peas and julienne of chicken breasts.

REYNIERE (1758–1838): Alexandre Balthazar Laurent Grimod de la Reyniere, writer and gourmet, famous for books in culinary arts such as *Almanachs des Gourmands* and *Manuels des Amphitryons.* Garniture for meat: Glazed chestnuts with little sausages, Madeira sauce, and chicken or calf liver.

RICHELIEU (1585–1642): Cardinal Armand Jean du Plessis de Richelieu, French statesman, fought Protestantism in France, founder of the Academie Francaise. Garniture for meat: Filet of beef with jus, garnished with stuffed mushrooms, filled tomatoes, braised lettuce, chateau potatoes.

ROHAN (1734–1803): Louis Rene Eduardo, Prince de Rohan, Cardinal and Archbishop of Strasbourg, famous because of his affairs with Queen

Marie Antoinette, famous gourmet. Honored with Chicken Rohan: Chicken sauté, garnished with filled artichoke bottoms with goose liver, tartlets with cock's combs and kidneys in Sauce Germain, white mushroom sauce, over chicken.

ROMANOFF: Romanoff Dynasty, rulers of Russia from 1613 to 1917, last Romanoff Emperor Nicolais II. Honored with Strawberries Romanoff: Strawberries marinated in port wine and sugar garnished with whipped cream.

ROSEBERRY (1847–1939): Archibald Philippe Primrose, fifth earl of Roseberry, British statesman. Garniture for meat: Stuffed tomatoes, croquettes filled with morels (French-type mushrooms), sautéed green beans, glazed cucumber balls, and beef jus.

ROSSINI (1792–1868): Gioachimov Antonio, Italian operatic composer, famous gourmet, well liked by the chefs of his circles. Famous for his truffle salad. One of his friends honored him with Tournedos Rossini: Filet of beef sauté, slice of pate de foie gras (goose liver), slice of truffle, covered with Madeira sauce.

ROSTAND (1869–1918): Edmond, French dramatist, famous for dramatic poetry "Aiglon" and "Cyrano de Bergerac." Garniture for meat: Diced artichokes, champignons in cream sauce, Sauce Colbert.

ROTHSCHILD: Name of the famous banker dynasty in Europe. The name derived from a rot (red) shield on the house in which the family lived in the ghetto of Frankfurt, Germany. Famous Chef Carême worked for Baronesse Rothschild, he created for her Soufflé Rothschild: Fill soufflé pan one-third with vanilla ice cream, cover with diced, fresh, Kirshwasser-liquor-marinated fruits, fill with vanilla soufflé batter and bake quickly.

RUBENS (1577–1640): Peter Paul, famous Dutch painter. Consommé Rubens: Chicken consommé with peeled, diced tomatoes and tapioca.

RUMFORD (1753–1814): Benjamin Thompson, count, British-American scientist, philanthropist, and administrator, was made count by Maximillian of Bavaria for his service to improve the social climate in his state. Soup Rumford was given away to the poor of the state (peas and potato soup with barley and bacon).

RUMOHR (1785–1843): Carl Frederic of Rumohr, historian famous for his literary work in the culinary arts, *Der Geist der Kochkunst* (The Spirit of the Culinary Art). Honored with Bavarian Cream Rumohr: Bavarian cream with almond milk and whipped cream; mixed with strawberries and Kirshwasser-liquor-marinated macaroons and pineapples.

SACHER (About 1830–1892): Eduardo, famous hotelier and owner of the Grand Hotel Sacher in Vienna, Austria. He created and gave his name to the Sacher Torte, a special chocolate cake with raspberry filling and covered with chocolate icing.

SAND (1804–1876): George, the pseudonym of Madame Amandine Lucile Aurore Dudevant, French novelist, friend of Chopin. Honored with the Filet of Sole George Sand: Sole poached in white wine court bouillon, fish dumplings, surrounded with prawns covered with Sauce Normande, which is mixed with shrimp butter.

SANDWICH (1718–1792): Fourth earl of Sandwich in England, postmaster general, secretary of state, First Lord of the Admiralty. He gave his name to the snack called "sandwich"—anything between two slices of bread.

SARAH BERNHARDT (1844–1923): Rosalie, French actress, member of the Comedie Française, one of the most famous actresses of her time. Escoffier created for her Consommé Sarah Bernhardt: Chicken consommé with tapioca, chicken dumplings mixed with shrimp butter, slices of beef marrow, green asparagus tips, and truffles. Filet of Sole Sarah Bernhardt: Poached, covered with shrimp sauce, surrounded with slices of lobster and truffles.

SAVARY (1774–1833): Anne Jean Marie Rene, Duke of Ravigo, French general and diplomat, also Minister Du Police for Napoleon I. Tournedos Savary: Filet of beef, garnished with tartlets of potato croquettes, filled with a puree of celery covered with Madeira sauce.

SCHUWALOW (1830–1908): Count Paul Adrejewitsch, Russian general, Russian ambassador in Berlin, gourmet. His chef created for him Chicken Soup Schuwalow: Chicken cream soup with shrimp puree and garnished with small shrimp.

SCRIBE (1791–1861): Augustin Eugene, famous French dramatist, he wrote every kind of drama—vaudevilles, comedies, tragedies, opera, libretti—more than 500 of them. Garniture for meat: Tartlets of rice with goose liver, truffles, and Madeira sauce.

SERGIUS: Sergius IV, pope from 1009–1012, had been known as "Pigmouth" before he was consecrated successor to Pope John XVIII. Garniture for meat: Sautéed cucumber filled with rice pilaf, Madeira sauce.

SEVIGNE (1626–1696): Marie De Rabutin-Chantial, Marquise of Sevigne, French letter-writer. Chicken Consommé Sevigne: Chicken consommé with chicken dumplings, green peas, and slices of stuffed lettuce. Garniture for meat: Stuffed lettuce champignons grille, Chateau potatoes, Madeira sauce.

SKOBELEW (1843–1882): Mikhail Dimitrievich, Russian general, honored with Ice Bombe Skobelew: Line out the form with vodka ice cream, fill inside with whipped cream mixed with cumin.

SOUBISE (1715–1787): Charles de Rohan, Prince of Soubise, peer and marshal of France, gourmet. His chef introduced white onion puree with rice; all dishes served with this onion puree are called "à la Soubise."

STAEL (1766–1817): Anne Louise Germaine Necker, Baronne de Stael-Holstein, French novelist and writer. Tournedos Stael: Sautéed beef set on chicken croquettes, topped with a champignon filled with champignon puree, covered with Madeira sauce surrounded with tartlets filled with green peas.

STANLEY (1841–1904): Sir Henri Morton, originally James Rowland, British explorer of Africa, discoverer of the course of the Congo. Poularde Stanley: Chicken filled with rice that is mixed with champignons and truffles, then cooked in a fond with onions; when cooked, mixed with chicken velouté; cover chicken with this sauce. Fish Stanley: Cooked set of pilaf rice covered with white wine sauce, garnished with champignon slices and truffles.

STROGANOFF (About 1700–1800): Russian businessman of Novgorod, later count, he had land behind the Ural, responsible for exploring and settling part of Siberia. Beef Stroganoff: Julienne of beef, sautéed, spiced with mustard and mixed with sour cream sauce.

SUCHET (1770–1826): Louis Gabrial, Duc D'Albufera Da Valencia, Marshal of France. Most brilliant general to Napoleon I, born to a silk manufacturer in Lyons, France. Filet of Sole Suchet: Sole poached with julienne of carrots, turnips, celery, leek, mixed with white wine sauce; cover the fish with this sauce and glaze.

TAILLEVENT (1326–1395): Guillaume Tirel, first chef on the Court for King Karl V and VI of France, writer of the first French cookbook, *Le Viandier*. Honored with Filet of Sole Taillevent: Sole poached, set on a puree of morels (mushrooms), covered with Mornay sauce, gratinée, surrounded with tartlets filled with fish puree.

TALLEYRAND-PERIGORD (1754–1838): Charles Maurice de Talleyrand, bishop, French diplomatist and statesman, famous French gastronome. Chicken Talleyrand: Roasted chicken filled with a mixture of finely chopped chicken breast, cut spaghetti, goose liver, truffles; bind with Mornay sauce, then cover the chicken with a light farce, put back in oven for a few minutes.

TOLSTOY (1828–1910): Count Leo Nikolayevich, Russian novelist, poet, and moral philosopher. Famous for his books *War and Peace* and *Anna Karenina*, which were made into movies. Sauté Beef Tolstoy: Sauté beef with diced tomatoes, onions, sour pickles; spiced with salt, pepper, paprika, and brown sauce.

TRAUTTMANNSDORF (1825–1870): Count T. Ferdinand, Austrian statesman. Honored with Rice Pudding Trauttmannsdorf: Sweet milk rice with vanilla, added gelatin, whipped cream and Maraschino liquor; fill in forms, chill, then take out of the forms and serve with a puree of fresh raspberries or raspberry syrup.

UXELLES (About 1700): Louis Chalor de Bled, Marquis D'Uxelles. His Chef Francois-Pierre de la Varenne created a mushroom farce called "Duxelles" consisting of mushrooms, onions, and shallots sautéed in butter spiced with salt, pepper, nutmeg.

VANDERBILT (1794–1877): Cornelius, American capitalist, made his money in railways. He endowed Vanderbilt University in Nashville, Tennessee. Lobster Vanderbilt: Ragout with lobsters, shrimps, truffles, and mushrooms in sauce Americaine, sometimes glazed on top.

VAN DYCK (1599–1641): Sir Anthony, famous Dutch painter. Honored with Chicken Sauté Van Dyck: Sautéed chicken with white wine glazed with cream, then covered with chicken cream sauce mixed with hop sprouts.

VATEL (1635–1676): François, Courtmaster (maître d' hôtel also cook) for Count of Conde, of Swiss parentage. A legend three centuries old presents Vatel to us as a great master in culinary fields of the Louis XIV era. Let us speak solely and briefly of Vatel, and ask ourselves whether the echo of Vatel's culinary genius would have come down to us without the witty gossip of Mme. Marie De Sevigne, written through her personal letters. Consommé Vatel: Fish consommé with julienne of sole, and a royale with shrimp puree. Filet of Sole Vatel: Poached sole, covered with Sauce Chambord, garnished with filled cucumbers and baked filet of sole.

VERDI (1813–1901): Giuseppe Fortunino Francesco, Italian composer, famous for his operas "Aida," "Falstaff," "Macbeth," and "Rigoletto" besides others. Sole Verdi: Sole cooked, put on diced, cooked macaroni, slices of lobster and truffles, covered with light cheese sauce, oven baked.

VILLARET (1750–1812): De Joyeuse Louis Thomas, French admiral, also governor general of Venice. Tournedos Villaret: Small grilled tournedos, set on tartlets filled with a puree of green beans, on top a champignon rosette, covered with Madeira sauce.

VILLARS (1653–1734): Claude Louis Hector de, Prince de Martignes, Marquis and Duc de Villars and Viscomte de Melun, Marshal of France, diplomat, one of the greatest generals of French history. Potage Villars: A puree soup from green beans, artichoke bottoms, onions, spices, finished with soft butter and heavy cream.

VILLEROI (1644–1730): Francois De Neufville, Duc De Villeroi, French marshall. His chef created Sauce Villeroi: Mushroom and truffles essence with Sauce Alemande; all dishes served with this sauce are called a la Villeroi.

WASHINGTON (1732–1799): George, general, statesman and first president of the United States. Chicken Washington: Roast chicken filled with corn a la Greek, served with chicken cream sauce with corn.

WELLINGTON (1769–1852): Arthus Welesley, first duke of Wellington, English field marshall, famous for his winning battles of Waterloo. Honored with Filet Wellington: Lightly roasted whole filet, cooled, covered with duxelles farce, surrounded with thin slices of bacon; put in pastry dough, bake, slice, serve with truffle sauce.

Proclamation

JOSEPH AMENDOLA

❋

Joseph Amendola,"Mr. A", ambassador, teacher, mentor,
author, consummate culinary professional:

For your nearly 50 years of dedication and service to
The Culinary Institute of America;

For your tireless efforts to assist CIA alumni and
students in career development;

For your pioneering spirit in helping to establish and
develop the educational programs at the CIA;

For your widely recognized contributions to the
foodservice and hospitality industry;

For your caring, unassuming manner which has made
you one of the most respected and beloved people in the
restaurant business

And in testimony to your outstanding leadership,
unwavering devotion to the culinary profession, and undying
commitment to the CIA's educational mission;

I hereby confer upon you the title Honorary Alumnus
of The Culinary Institute of America with all the rights
and privileges pertaining thereto and ask that Alumni
Committee member Phyllis Flaherty present this bronze sculp-
ture replica of the Bocuse d'Or Toque in testimony thereof.

May 19, 1997

Robert E. Walker

Robert E. Walker '68
Chairman,
Alumni Committee

Reader's Notes and Thoughts

Reader's Notes and Thoughts

Reader's Notes and Thoughts